Great American Holiday Cookbook

*Their History and Wonderful
Recipes to Celebrate*

Susie Federer

GREAT AMERICAN HOLIDAY COOKBOOK
—Their History and Wonderful Recipes to Celebrate
by Susie Federer

COOKING / AMERICAN HISTORY
ISBN: 978-1-7369590-2-2

Cover design by Jennifer S. Goins

Amerisearch, Inc., P.O. Box 60442, Fort Myers, FL 33906
1-888-USA-WORD
www.AmericanMinute.com, smfederer@gmail.com

Bless the food before us,
the family beside us, and
the love between us!
Amen!

❧

"Jesus said unto them, 'Come and dine.' And none of the disciples dared ask him, Who are you? knowing that it was the Lord."

–John 21:12

CONTENTS

❧
DEDICATION

I dedicate this book to my beautiful family! First of all, my husband Bill who I have been cooking for over 40 years. I won his heart while dating by cooking for him.

And to my children who were my inspiration for making healthy delicious meals and snacks. We really enjoyed baking for the holidays as evidenced by all the yummy dessert recipes. I would love to see the smile on their faces when they ate something wonderful that I had made just for them.

A special thank you to my lovely sister-in-laws whose holiday recipes I included. We had so much fun when gathering with Bill's ten brothers and sisters and their families for the holidays. Fantastic food was brought by everyone.

And I thank God for the blessing of growing up in America where there is a bounty of good fresh food.

May God bless you and continue to bless America.

— Susie Federer, 2022

Great American Holiday Cookbook – Susie Federer

∞

CHRISTMAS EVE

"The next day, John the Baptist saw Jesus coming toward him, and said, 'Behold! The Lamb of God who takes away the sin of the world!'"

– John 1:29

In the 8th century before Christ, the Prophet Isaiah wrote (7:14):

Therefore the Lord himself shall give you a sign; Behold, a virgin shall conceive, and bear a son, and shall call his name Immanuel.

The Gospel of Matthew, 1:20–23, relates:

The angel of the Lord appeared unto him in a dream, saying, Joseph, thou son of David, fear not to take unto thee Mary thy wife: for that which is conceived in her is of the Holy Ghost. And she shall bring forth a son, and thou shalt call his name Jesus: for he shall save his people from their sins.

And when King Herod had

gathered all the chief priests and scribes of the people together, he demanded of them where Christ should be born. And they said unto him, in Bethlehem of Judea: for thus it is written by the prophet,

"And thou Bethlehem, in the land of Judea, art not the least among the princes of Judea: for out of thee shall come a Governor, that shall rule my people Israel" ...

Now all this was done, that it might be fulfilled which was spoken of the Lord by the prophet, saying,

"Behold, a virgin shall be with child, and shall bring forth a son, and they shall call his name Emmanuel, which being interpreted is, God with us."

On Christmas Eve, 1946, Truman said:

Our ... hopes of future years turn to a little town in the hills of Judea where on a winter's night two thousand years ago the prophecy of Isaiah was fulfilled.

Shepherds keeping the

watch by night over their flock heard the glad tidings of great joy from the angels of the Lord singing, "Glory to God in the Highest and on Earth, peace, good will toward men."

The Apostle Paul wrote Galatians, 4:4–5:

When the time had fully come, God sent forth his Son, born of woman, born under the law, to redeem those who were under the law so that we might receive adoption as sons.

On Christmas Eve, 1947, President Truman lit the National Christmas Tree, saying:

The angels sang for joy at the first Christmas in faraway Bethlehem. Their song has echoed through the corridors of time and will continue to sustain the heart of man through eternity ... A humble man and woman had gone up from Galilee out of the City of Nazareth to Bethlehem.

On Christmas Eve, 1952, Truman stated while lighting the National Christmas Tree:

Then a Child was born in a stable. A star hovered over, drawing wise men from afar. Shepherds, in a field, heard angels singing ... That was the first Christmas and it was God's great gift to us ...

Year after year it brings peace and tranquility to troubled hearts in a troubled world. And tonight the earth seems hushed, as we turn to the old, old story of how "God so loved the world, that He gave His only begotten Son, that whosoever believeth in Him should not perish, but have everlasting life" ...

Let us remember always to try to act and live in the spirit of the Prince of Peace. He bore in His heart no hate and no malice – nothing but love for all mankind ...

Through Jesus Christ the world will yet be a better and a fairer place ... I wish for all of you a Christmas filled with the joy of the Holy Spirit, and many years of future happiness with the peace of God reigning upon this earth.

After his first year in office, President Donald Trump lit the National Christmas Tree, November 20, 2017, stating:

There's hardly an aspect of our lives today that His life has not touched: art, music, culture, law, and our respect for the sacred dignity of every person everywhere in the world.

Each and every year at Christmas time we recognize that the real spirit of Christmas is not what we have, it's about who we are – each one of us is a child of God. That is the true source of joy this time of the year. Jesus Christ inspires us to love one another with hearts full of generosity and grace.

On Christmas Eve, 1983, President Ronald Reagan addressed the nation via radio:

Some celebrate Christmas as the birthday of a great teacher and philosopher.

But to other millions of us, Jesus is much more. He is divine, living assurance that God so loved the world He gave us His only begotten Son so that by believing in Him and learning to love each other we could one day be together in paradise.

❦

Great American Holiday Cookbook – Susie Federer

❧

CHRISTMAS EVE RECIPES

Here are some of my family's favorite Christmas recipes for you to enjoy leading up to Christmas Eve.

❧

BEST GINGERBREAD MEN EVER

You can make the dough ahead of time and freeze it until you are ready to roll the cookies out, bake and decorate!

1. Preheat oven to 325 degrees.
2. In a large bowl with a mixer, combine:
   1 cup of butter or margarine softened.

1 cup of light brown sugar firmly packed.

2 eggs.

1/2 cup of unsulfured molasses.

Beat 2 minutes until well blended.

3. Gradually add in:

5 ½ cups of all–purpose flour.

2 teaspoons of baking soda.

2 teaspoons of ground cinnamon.

1 teaspoon of ground nutmeg.

1 teaspoon of ginger.

1/2 teaspoon of ground cloves (optional).

Separate dough into 4 large balls and chill in a covered bowl for one hour.

4. Cover a pastry cloth first with flour and then white sugar. Spread it around and also cover rolling pin with mixture.

5. Roll a ball of dough out at a time and use cookie cutters to make gingerbread men, angels, stars, bell and trees to decorate.

6. Place equal sized shapes on greased cookie sheets and bake for 6–7 minutes on 2 centered oven racks.

7. Switch racks and bake 6–7 minutes more until done. Edges should not be overly brown

8. Cool completely and then decorate with white icing and we use M&Ms and sprinkles.

9. Decorator buttercream frosting: cream 1/2 cup butter and shortening and add 1 ½ teaspoon clear vanilla extract and dash of salt.

Add 5 cups confectioners' sugar a cup at

a time beating on medium speed.

Add 2–3 tablespoons of milk, one tablespoon at a time on high until blended and piping consistency. Spoon into piping bag and decorate.

❧

GRAMMY'S HOLLY COOKIES

Bill wanted me to add Grammy's Holly Cookies. He is the 5th of 11 children and this is an easy fun recipe that he and his siblings could make together. His Mom, "Grammy" loved these cookies.

1. Melt 1 stick of butter in a large saucepan.

2. Add one 10 ½ ounce bag of miniature marshmallows and keep stirring until melted.

3. Add 1 teaspoon vanilla and 2 teaspoons of green food coloring.

4. Quickly stir in 4 cups of corn flakes until coated with the marshmallow mix.

5. Place spoonfuls on wax paper and top each with 3 cinnamon candies to look like holly berries.

6. I sprinkle a little green sprinkles on top to make them look more festive. Have fun getting sticky making these!

❦
SAINT NICHOLAS

'T was the night before Christmas, when all through the house, Not a creature was stirring, not even a mouse; The stockings were hung by the chimney with care, In hopes that St. Nicholas soon would be there!

– Rev. Clement Moore, *A Visit from St. Nicholas,* 1823

The true story of Saint Nicholas, or as the Dutch pronounced his name "Santa Claus," began with the Greek Orthodox tradition.

Saint Nicholas was born around AD 280, the only child of a wealthy, elderly couple who lived in Patara, Asia Minor (present–day Turkey). When his parents died in a plague, Nicholas inherited their wealth. He generously gave to the poor, but he did so anonymously, as he wanted the glory to go to God.

In the 3rd century, a pietist movement spread where sincere converts to Christianity would give away all their money and possessions, then withdraw from the world to live as a hermit in a cave or join a monastery.

One notable incident in Nicholas' life

was when a merchant in his town had gone bankrupt. The creditors threatened to take not only his property, but also his children.

The merchant had three daughters, he did not want them taken by the creditors, so he had the idea of quickly marrying them off. Unfortunately, he did not have money for the dowry, which was needed in that area of the world for a legally recognized wedding.

Nicholas heard of his dilemma and late one night, threw a bag of money in the window for the oldest daughter's dowry. Supposedly the bag of money landed in a shoe or a stocking that was drying by the fireplace. It was the talk of the town.

Nicholas then threw a bag of money in the window for the second daughter, and she was able to get married. Expecting money for his third daughter, the merchant waited up. When Nicholas threw the money in, the father ran outside and caught him.

Nicholas made the father promise not to tell where the money came from, as he wanted the credit to go to God alone. This was the origin of secret, midnight gift–giving and hanging stockings by the fireplace on the anniversary of Saint Nicholas' death, which was December 6, 343 AD.

(Get the book, *There Really is a Santa Claus–History of Saint Nicholas & Christmas Holiday Traditions.*)

≪◌

❧

CHRISTMAS DAY RECIPES

W e usually had a nice brunch and then joined other Federers for an extended family dinner. These are two of our favorite brunch recipes.

❧

BREAKFAST FRITTATA

1. Preheat oven to 350 degrees.

2. In a large skillet, that you can also heat in the oven, brown 2 small grated red potatoes and ¼ of a sweet yellow onion in a tablespoon

of olive oil until lightly browned.

3. Whisk 6 eggs and 1/4 cup milk (I use 2% but you can use whole milk or cream.)

4. Chop 1/2 of a 9 ounce bag of fresh spinach into very small pieces and sprinkle over the potatoes and onion.

5. Pour the milk and egg mixture over that. And top with as much grated Colby–Jack or feta cheese as you like. The kids prefer Colby–Jack.

6. You can slice fresh little cocktail tomatoes on top to give it that Christmas look or use some sundried tomatoes. We slice jalapenos on top of 1/2 for those who like heat.

7. Bake at 350 for about 20–30 minutes and serve with fresh salsa on the side.

8. You can substitute the spinach with chopped asparagus and you can also stir in cooked small pieces of bacon or turkey bacon for extra flavor.

9. Finish the brunch with warm Christmas Cranberry Bread.

❧

CHRISTMAS CRANBERRY BREAD

1. Preheat oven to 350 degrees. You can bake this along with the frittata. It may take a little longer and will be a perfect finish to the frittata.

2. Combine the dry ingredients:

2 cups flour.

3/4 cups sugar.

1 ½ teaspoon baking powder.

1 teaspoon baking soda

3. With blender, beat the next ingredients until smooth:

1 softened 3 ounce cream cheese. You can use light cream cheese.

1/2 cup warm milk.

1/2 cup melted butter.

2 teaspoons lemon juice.

2 teaspoons vanilla.

2 large eggs.

3. Beat in the dry ingredients. Then stir in 1 to 1 ½ cups of fresh or frozen cranberries. Bake in greased bundt pan 1 hour or until fork comes out clean.

4. Cool 10–15 minutes and turn onto a festive platter and enjoy warm.

❧

FAMOUS ARTICHOKE SPINACH DIP

For extended Federer family Christmas dinners, each sister would bring a favorite, such as brisket, shrimp cocktail, meatballs, turkey, veggie trays, salads, sides, and cookie platters. I was always asked to bring my delicious artichoke spinach dip!

1. Preheat oven to 375 degrees.

2. Combine the following ingredients in a bowl:

13 ounce can of artichoke hearts, drained and chopped fine.

10 ounce package frozen spinach, thawed, squeezed dry and chopped fine or one 10 ounce bag of fresh spinach chopped fine.

1 cup mayonnaise – can be light.

1 cup freshly grated Parmesan cheese. (You can use the canned grated Parmesan instead).

2 cups grated Monterey or Colby–Jack cheese.

3. Pour into 1 quart baking dish. I use a pretty oval red dish for the holidays.

5. I top 1/2 with sundried tomatoes and one half with sliced fresh jalapenos, but that is not necessary. Then top with 1/2 cup more grated cheese.

6. Bake in the middle of the oven until cheese is melted. About 15–20 minutes depending on the baking dish.

7. Place baking dish and serving tray and surround with your choice of crackers or tortilla or blue corn chips.

❦

NEW YEAR'S EVE

The famous song "Auld Lang Syne," (meaning "in days of old gone by") was written in 1788 by poet Robert Burns. It is sung on New Year's Eve around the world.

The phrase "for auld lang syne" essentially boils down to "for old time's sake." It is a reflective call to preserve our oldest, dearest friendships with generous forgiveness, overlooking past wrongs.

New Year's Eve is a time when people come together to recall the joys and sorrows of years past, specifically those spent in each other's company:

Should old acquaintance be forgot,
and never brought to mind?
Should old acquaintance be forgot,
and old lang syne?
CHORUS:
For auld lang syne, my dear,
for auld lang syne,
we'll take a cup of kindness yet,
for auld lang syne.

A similar poem was written by Henry Wadsworth Longfellow in 1881, titled "Auf Wiedersehen" (meaning "until we meet again"). Longfellow dedicated it to the memory of his friend James T. Fields.

The poem alluded to the Bible verse in Hebrews 11 "By faith ... women received their dead raised to life again," and that Heaven is where we will see our friends again forever:

Until we meet again!
That is the meaning of the familiar words, that men repeat
when parting in the streets.
Ah yes, till then!
But when death intervening
Rends us asunder,
With what ceaseless pain
We wait for the Again! ...
Believing, in the midst of our afflictions,
That death is a beginning, not an end,
We cry to them, and send
Farewells,
that better might be called predictions,
Being fore–shadowings of the future, thrown
Into the vast Unknown.
Faith overleaps the confines of
our reason,
And if by faith, as in old times was said,
Women received their dead
Raised up to life, then only for a season
Our partings are, nor shall we wait in vain
Until we meet again!

On New Year's Eve many gather to pray for a blessed New Year. Here is my prayer:

Dear Heavenly Father, We thank you for this time on earth to do Your Will. We thank you for the blessings of the past year. We pray that You bless our country, our church, our family and friends this New Year. Protect our Nation. Give us godly leaders who will listen to your voice and do Your Will without cowardice.

We repent for the sins of our nation. We pray for life and liberty for all, born and unborn. Do not let plagues or wars come upon us. Keep us in good health. We thank You for your prosperity and ask that you lead us to use it wisely to promote your Kingdom on earth.

We thank you that Your Son Jesus came to earth as an example to us and died to open the doors to heaven for us. We cover ourselves, our family and our children with the blood of Jesus. We thank you that we will follow His example and lead others to You this Year.

We love You Lord and rededicate our lives to you this New Year. Holy Spirit, rise up within us, your church and give us strength to do God's Will here on earth this New Year. We thank You and Praise You, Our Heavenly Father. In Jesus' Mighty Name, Amen.

A nice family activity is to have each family member list ten New Year's Resolutions!

On New Year's Eve, many people like to enjoy Chinese food. In many Asian countries, everyone celebrates their birthday on New Year's. We like to make our own Chinese dishes with lots of veggies and very little fat.

&

HOMEMADE EGG ROLLS
This is our daughter's favorite.

1. Finely chop 1/3 of a head of green cabbage and mix with finely grated carrots. Add as much as you want of chopped shrimp or chopped cooked chicken.

2. Put a spoonful onto a wonton wrapper

and roll from corner to corner. Tuck the corners in and wet the last corner with a little water to make them stay closed.

3. Cover the bottom of a frying pan with oil and heat. We use olive oil for the health benefits.

4. Carefully place the egg rolls in the pan. Brown on one side for about 2–3 minutes and turn until egg roll is browned all around.

5. Drain on paper towels and place on platter with sweet sour sauce and hot mustard for dipping. Enjoy warm. My kids love these homemade!

෴

MANDARIN SALAD

1. Chop leafy green lettuce and spinach or spring mix and place in large bowl.

2. Garnish with grated carrots and sliced cucumbers.

3. Pour the juice from a can of mandarin oranges in small bowl and add balsamic vinegar to taste. Salt and pepper to taste.

4. Top salad with mandarin oranges and slivered almonds.

5. Pour dressing on top according to taste.

❧

STIR FRY FUN

1. Prepare 1–2 cups Jasmine Rice according to package instructions.

2. Heat a little oil (can be sesame or olive oil if you like) in frying pan or wok if you have one and warm.

3. Add peeled shrimp or chicken tenders and/or even thinly sliced steak to hot oil.

4. Next add snow peas, thinly sliced

carrots, zucchini, onion and celery and drained sliced water chestnuts if desired.

5. We also toss in pineapple tidbits and cashews and stir fry quickly. Do not overcook.

6. Top or serve with teriyaki or soy sauce, over Jasmine rice.

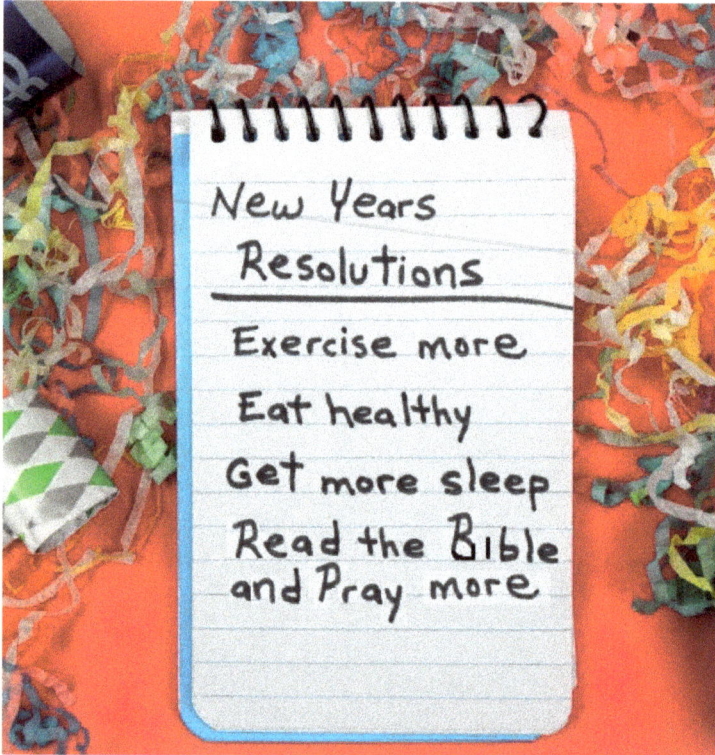

Great American Holiday Cookbook – Susie Federer

✑
NEW YEAR'S DAY

Therefore if any man be in Christ, he is a new creature: old things are passed away; behold, all things are become new."

– 2 Corinthians 5:17

Julius Caesar moved the beginning of the year to January 1st. The Julian calendar and the Gregorian calendar both observe this day.

The Roman month of January was named after Janus, their deity of gateways and beginnings. In Asia, New Year's Day is a major celebration, with many countries having everyone turn a year older on that day.

Many Americans celebrate by gathering with family and friends to watch football games or just enjoy the day off together.

My Hungarian grandmother would make a big pot of homemade cabbage rolls and keep them warm on the stove for guests to enjoy while visiting. Then she would serve homemade pies and cookies.

❧

STUFFED CABBAGE ROLLS

1. Make one to 2 cups cooked rice.

2. Cook one pound of ground beef in frying pan with 1/2 medium chopped yellow onion and one chopped clove of garlic. Drain the grease from the beef. Salt and pepper to taste.

3. Add 1/2 cup of cooked rice and one 8 ounce can of tomato sauce.

4. Cut the core out of a head of cabbage and submerge in big pot of boiling water for 3–5 minutes. Then with a cooking tong pull leaves off the cabbage one at a time being careful not to tear them and place them on a plate to cool.

5. Take a large leaf of cabbage and stuff it with about 2 tablespoons of the meat and rice mixture.

6. Roll it like a burrito stuffing the ends

in well so the filling does not leak out.

7. Leave about an inch of water in the pot that you boiled the cabbage in and start placing the cabbage rolls in the water. You can layer them on top of each other.

8. When you get to the little whiter leaves in the center, you can just slice them in ribbons and lay on top of the rolls. Top with one can of diced tomatoes and simmer on low for about 40 minutes. Turn stove top to warm and enjoy whenever guests arrive.

9. An easier version for Moms in a hurry is to just chop all the cabbage as ribbons, add some grated carrots and a little more tomato sauce and serve as a healthy soup. You can season with paprika, turmeric or even Italian seasonings that you like.

BLACK–EYED PEA SALAD
Many people like to eat black–eyed peas on New Year's. We like them in this fun salad!

1. Drain 1 can (15 1/2 ounces each) black–eyed peas, rinsed and drained.

2. Add 2 cups grape tomatoes, halved.

3. Add 1 each finely chopped small green and red peppers.

4. Add 1 small red onion, chopped and 1 celery stalk finely chopped.

5. I add 2 tablespoons minced fresh basil oregano and chopped chives from my herb garden.

6. Pour DRESSING over salad.

7. 1/4 cup red wine vinegar or balsamic vinegar.

8. Add a pinch of your favorite hot sauce.

3/4 teaspoon salt.

1/2 teaspoon freshly ground pepper.

1/4 cup olive oil.

&

LITTLE PECAN AND CHERRY PIES

Little pecan and cherry pies for dessert was my grandmother's recipe.

1. Mix one stick of butter or margarine and one 3 ounce package of cream cheese at room temperature with one cup of flour. Put in refrigerator to chill while making filling.

2. Beat 1 egg with 3/4 cup of brown sugar, 1 tablespoon of melted butter, and 1 tablespoon of vanilla.

3. Then add 1 cup of crushed pecans.

4. Fill greased miniature cupcake pans with dough and make a center for the filling with your fingers. Make it look like a little pie crust.

5. Fill center with about 1 teaspoon of filling.

6. Bake at 350 for 25 minutes. Cool 5–10 minutes and gently take out of pan.

7. You can also use canned cherry pie filling.

Rev. Martin Luther King, Jr. Day

❧

REV. MARTIN LUTHER KING, JR. DAY

"**I** have a dream ... where little black boys and black girls will be able to join hands with little white boys and white girls and walk together as sisters and brothers"

– Rev. Dr. Martin Luther King, Jr., August 28, 1963, at the Civil Rights March in Washington, D.C.

Rev. King stood on principles found in the Holy Bible. His dream was the continuation of the Founding Fathers' dream that "All men are created equal and endowed by their Creator with certain unalienable rights."

He delivered his famous "I have a dream" speech in front of the Lincoln memorial in Washington DC, declaring,

When the Architects of our Republic wrote the magnificent words of the Constitution and the Declaration of Independence, they were signing a promissory note to which every American was to fall heir.

Today, his statue stands between the Lincoln Memorial and Jefferson Memorial.

Martin Luther King, Jr. attended Booker T. Washington High School in Atlanta, Georgia, 1942–1944.

Booker T. Washington founded the Tuskegee Institute in Alabama. He wrote in *Up From Slavery* (1901):

> I learned this lesson from General Samuel Chapman Armstrong, and resolved that I would permit no man, no matter what his color might be, to narrow and degrade my soul by making me hate him.

> With God's help, I believe that I have completely rid myself of any ill feeling toward the Southern white man for any wrong that he may have inflicted upon my race.

> I am made to feel just as happy now when I am rendering service to Southern white men as when the service is rendered to a member of my own race ...

> I pity from the bottom of my heart any individual who is so unfortunate as to get into the habit of holding race prejudice.

Booker T. Washington stated:

In the sight of God there is no color line, and we want to cultivate a spirit that will make us forget that there is such a line anyway.

I have always had the greatest respect for the work of the Salvation Army especially because I have noted that it draws no color line in religion.

Rev. Martin Luther King, Jr. who was a Baptist Pastor like his father and grandfather, said at the Civil Rights March, August 28, 1963:

Now is the time to open the doors of opportunity to all of God's children ...

I have a dream that one day ... the glory of the Lord shall be revealed, and all flesh shall see it together.

This will be the day when all of God's children will be able to sing with new meaning, "My country 'tis of thee, Sweet land of liberty, Of thee I sing."

Rev. Martin Luther King, Jr. stated:

We must not allow our creative protest to degenerate

into violence ...

For there is the more excellent way of LOVE.

୶

SOUTHERN FRIED CHICKEN

1. Heat 1 cup oil or shortening in large cast iron skillet over medium high heat.

2. In a brown paper lunch bag, combine 2 cups of flour, 1 teaspoon of black pepper, 1 teaspoon of paprika, and 1 teaspoon of salt.

Use 2–3 pounds of whole chickens cut into pieces or already cut thighs, legs and breasts.

Shake 2 pieces in the bag at a time starting with larger pieces like the breasts and place them in the hot oil in skillet.

Repeat until all chicken is coated and in the skillet.

3. Fry the chicken over medium–high heat until all pieces have browned on both sides.

Then turn the heat to medium–low, and cover. Cook for about 25 minutes.

4. Remove the lid and increase heat to medium–high.

Fry until chicken is a deep golden brown.

❧

MIXED GREENS

1. Pull the leaves off of 2 bunches of collard greens, 2 bunches of turnip greens and 2 bunches of mustard greens. Discard the stems. Gently wash the greens in warm water to remove all the sand and soil.

2. Partially fill a clean sink with warm

water and stir in 3 tablespoons of salt and 2 cups of chicken broth. Soak the greens in the mixture for 10 minutes.

3. Scoop up the greens and drain them in a colander. Do not rinse them. Discard sink mixture.

4. Pour 2 fresh cups of chicken broth into a large pot and mix in the greens.

5. Stir in 1/2 cup of vegetable oil, 2 cloves of diced garlic, 1/2 cup cooked chopped bacon, 1/2 cup white sugar and salt and pepper to taste.

6. Bring to a boil and reduce heat to a simmer.

Cook about 45 minutes to an hour until greens are tender.

❧

SWEET POTATO PIE
1. Preheat oven to 325 degrees.
2. In the bowl of your electric mixer, 2–3 peeled roasted or boiled and mashed

sweet potatoes (or 1 ½ cups of canned sweet potatoes, mashed) with 1/2 cup of sugar, 2 large eggs, 4 tablespoons or 1/2 stick of softened butter, 1/4 cup of milk, 1 teaspoon of vanilla extract, 1/4 teaspoon of nutmeg, 1/2 teaspoon of cinnamon and a pinch of salt to taste. Beat well until blended and smooth.

3. Pour the mixture into one 9 inch pie shell, homemade or store bought and sprinkle with 1/4 cup of sugar. Let stand for 15 minutes before baking.

4. Bake at 325 degrees about one hour or until fork comes out clean and cool before serving.

∽

HOMEMADE PIE CRUST

For one crust:

1. In a large bowl, combine 1 1/4 cup all purpose flour with 1/8 teaspoon salt

2. In a small bowl combine 1/4 cup of vegetable oil or softened butter with 3 tablespoons of cold water. Pour this into flour mixture.

For Two Crusts Use

2 1/3 cups of flour, 1/4 teaspoon salt, 1/2 cup of oil or butter and 6 tablespoons of cold water.

3. Add to the flour all at once and stir lightly with a fork just until moistened.

4. If necessary, you can add up to 1 additional tablespoon water.

5. Form the dough into one or two balls. Flatten one ball into a pie dish and crimp the edges.

6. Place the dough ball for the top crust between 2 sheets of waxed paper and roll out.

Take off wax paper and trim crust to 1/2 inch beyond the edge of the pie plate.

Fold under the bottom crust and crimp after filling the pie.

Take a knife and poke about 6 spaced little holes in the top crust.

7. Bake as directed on pie recipe.

❧
SAINT VALENTINE'S DAY

"Greater love hath no man than this, that a man lay down his life for his friends."

— John 15:13

Saint Valentine is mentioned in *Legenda Sanctorum* by Jacobus de Voragine in 1260 and in the *Nuremberg Chronicle*, 1493.

Though several individuals may have had that name, it appears Saint Valentine was either a priest in Rome or a bishop in Terni, central Italy.

He risked the Emperor's wrath by standing up for traditional marriage, secretly marrying soldiers to their young brides.

When Emperor Claudius demanded that Christians deny their consciences and worship pagan idols, Saint Valentine refused. He was arrested, dragged before the Prefect of Rome, and condemned to die.

While awaiting execution, his jailer, Asterius, asked Saint Valentine to pray for his blind daughter. When she miraculously regained her sight, the jailer converted and was baptized, along with many others.

Right before his execution, Saint Valentine wrote a note to the jailer's daughter, signing it, "from your Valentine."

In 496 AD, Pope Gelasius designated February 14th as "Saint Valentine's Day."

After Chaucer poems, more references appeared in literature associating Saint Valentine's Day with courtly love.

This eventually developed into the 18th–century English traditions of presenting flowers, offering confectionery, and sending St. Valentine's Day greeting cards.

People often sign Valentine cards with X's and O's. The Greek name for Christ, Χριστό, begins with the letter "X" which in Greek is called "Chi." "X" became a common abbreviation for the name Christ. This is why Christ–mas is abbreviated as X–mas.

In Medieval times, the "X" was called the Christ's Cross, or "Criss–Cross." It reminded students that the fear of the Lord is the beginning of wisdom":

> Mortals ne'er shall know,
> More than contained of old the
> Chris'–cross row.

The Christ's Cross was a form of a written oath, the origin of signing at the X.

Similar to the ancient practice of swearing upon a Bible, saying "so help me God," then kissing the Bible, people would sign a document with or next to the Christ's Cross to swear before God they would keep the agreement, then kiss it to show sincerity.

Take this day to sincerely let those you

love, know how much you love them! Bill's father would write each of his eleven children a personal encouraging Valentine every year. He still remembers that today.

We do the same with each of our 4 children and 3 grandchildren. I also try to send or give a loving note and something sweet like a cupcake or cookies to the widows around me who seem lonely. It means so much to them.

❧

LOVELY HOLIDAY SALAD

1. Toss 4 cups of Boston or Bib or Spring Greens lettuce with one small can of drained mandarin oranges or you can use fresh clementines and one half cup of sweetened dried cranberries.

2. Add 1/2 cup of sliced green onions.

3. Mix 1/4 cup of cranberry juice cocktail,

2 tablespoons of olive oil, 1 teaspoon of honey, 1 tablespoon of red wine vinegar, salt and pepper to taste and pour over salad

4. Top with 1/2 cup of glazed pecans found in the baking aisle!

∾

FAVORITE SALMON DINNER

This is our family's favorite.

1.Cover large baking sheet or large glass baking dish that size with olive oil.

2. Place a fresh piece of salmon – I get one big enough to feed 4–6 people skin side down into pan.

3. Bake at 400 degrees for 15 minutes.

4. While it is baking, cut 3–4 tomatoes in half and dip cut side in melted butter. Top with a generous spoonful of Parmesan cheese and Canadian steak seasoning or just pepper.

5. Pull the salmon out of the oven and cover it with Raspberry Chipotle Sauce, Jerk Sauce, or slice pineapple. We prefer Raspberry Chipotle. It looks and tastes so good.

6. Surround the salmon with fresh baby spinach leaves and place tomatoes on top of the spinach.

7. Drizzle a little of the melted butter on the spinach and sprinkle a little Parmesan.

8. Broil all of it for 5 to 7 minutes until the sauce and tomatoes get a little browned.

9. Serve over Rice Pilaf, Chicken Rice-A-Roni, or Fettuccine and enjoy.

It makes a lovely presentation.

᪥

HUG COOKIES MADE EASY

You can use your favorite chocolate cookie dough recipe or your favorite brownie mix to make HUG COOKIES.

1. Preheat oven to 350 degrees.

2. I use one box Ghirardelli brownie mix with 2 eggs. Mix well.

3. Use a cookie scoop or roll into small balls and drop on baking sheet sprayed with coconut oil.

4. Bake 8–10 minutes according to size.

5. Cool 2 minutes and then press a Hershey's hug into cookie!

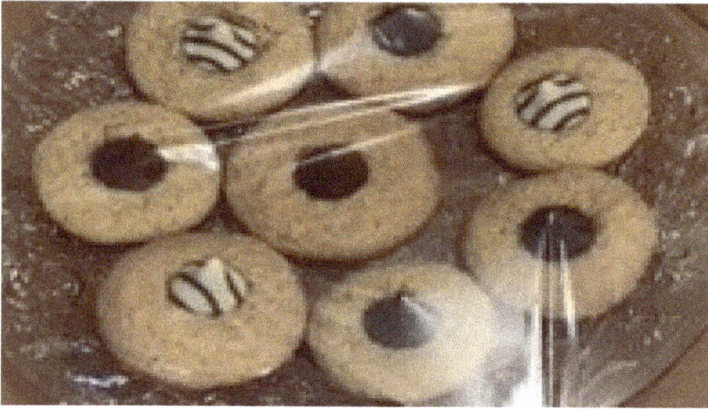

❧

KISS COOKIES

You can use ready–made peanut butter cookie dough from the refrigerator section to make KISS COOKIES

1. In large bowl, beat 1/2 cup of butter or shortening with 3/4 cup peanut butter.

2. Add 1/3 cup light brown sugar and 1 egg. Slowly mix in 2 tablespoons of milk and 1 teaspoon of vanilla.

3. Add in 1 ½ cup of flour and 1 teaspoon of baking soda, 1/2 teaspoon of salt.

4. Scoop with cookie scoop or roll about 2 teaspoon size balls and roll in granulated sugar.

5. Place ball on cookie sheet sprayed with coconut oil and bake 8–10 minutes until lightly browned.

6. Cool 1–2 minutes and press a dark or milk chocolate kiss into the middle.

7. Serve with hug cookies perfect for Valentines Day!

∽

PRESIDENTS' DAY

In 1783, while getting his portrait painted, King George III asked painter Benjamin West what Washington planned to do now that he had won the Revolution.

West replied: "They say he will return to his farm."

The King exclaimed: "If he does that, he will be the greatest man in the world."

Presidents' Day is actually George Washington's birthday, February 22, 1732.

In a world where kings killed to get power, kings killed to keep power, Washington had power, and gave it up!

Poet Robert Frost once wrote:

I often say of George Washington that he was one of the few men in the whole history of the worlds who was not carried away by power.

Charles Francis Adams, grandson of John Adams, wrote:

More than all, and above

all, Washington was master of himself. If there be one quality more than another in his character which may exercise a useful control over the men of the present hour, it is the total disregard of self when in the most elevated positions for influence and example.

George Washington was:

- unanimously chosen as the Army's Commander–in–Chief;

- unanimously chosen as President of the Constitutional Convention;

- unanimously chosen as the first U.S. President;

- unanimously re–elected to a second term.

Washington's Birthday was recognized by an Act of Congress for government offices in Washington, D.C., in 1879, and for all federal offices in 1885.

In 1971, the Uniform Monday Holiday Act to create more three–day weekends moved the observance of Washington's birthday to the third Monday in February.

Since Abraham Lincoln was also born in February, many States began to include him in the observance. This led still other States include all the Presidents in the observance.

After the Battle of the Monongahela,

Washington wrote from Fort Cumberland to his younger brother, John Augustine Washington, July 18, 1755:

> By the All–Powerful Dispensations of Providence, I have been protected beyond all human probability or expectation; for I had four bullets through my coat, and two horses shot under me, yet escaped unhurt, although death was leveling my companions on every side of me!

Washington addressed the Delaware Indian Chiefs who had brought youths to be trained in American schools, May 12, 1779:

> You do well to wish to learn our arts and ways of life, and above all, the religion of Jesus Christ.

In 1789, he was sworn in as the first President of the United States. On October 3, 1789, he thanked God for the Constitution:

> Whereas it is the duty of all nations to acknowledge the Providence of Almighty God ...

> I do recommend ... rendering unto Him our sincere and humble thanks, for ... the favorable interpositions of His

Providence ... we experienced in the course and conclusion of the late war ... for the peaceable and rational manner in which we have been enabled to establish constitutions of government.

In his Farewell Address, 1796, Washington warned:

Disorders and miseries, which result, gradually incline the minds of men to seek security and repose in the absolute power of an Individual ... (who) turns this disposition to the purposes of his own elevation, on the ruins of Public Liberty ...

The spirit of encroachment tends to consolidate the powers of all the departments in one, and thus to create, whatever the form of government, a real despotism ...

Let there be no change by usurpation; for though this, in one instance, may be the instrument of good, it is the customary weapon by which free governments are destroyed.

(Get the book, *Prayers and Presidents– Inspiring Faith From Leaders of the Past.*)

∾

SPINACH ARTICHOKE SALAD

1 small head of radicchio.

1 10 ounce bag of baby of spinach leaves.

2 vine–ripened tomatoes cut into wedges.

1 can of artichoke hearts drained and diced.

1/2 small red onion peeled and diced.

1/2 cup prepared light Italian salad dressing (like Newman's own).

Place radicchio and spinach leaves on a platter. Arrange tomato wedges on leaves to form flowers.

In large bowl toss artichoke hearts, red onion and Italian dressing until blended.

Drizzle mixture over salad. Toss lightly just before serving if desired.

Makes six servings.

❧

ROAST BEEF IN THE CROCK-POT

1. Brush inside of Crock-Pot with olive oil.

2. Place roast in Crock-Pot.

3. Pour red wine to cover bottom over Crock-Pot to tenderize it as it cooks.

4. Pour enough Worcestershire over roast to cover top. Sprinkle meat tenderizer and pepper over top of roast. I pour a little Barbeque sauce on top also.

5. Slice 1/2 or 1 onion depending on taste and size of roast and place on top. Cut medium size red potatoes in ½ and place around roast and if need be, on top of roast.

6. Top with one bag of baby carrots or carrots sliced in sticks. Top with one bag of fresh green beans, washed and trimmed.

7. Cook on high for 4–6 hours depending on size of roast. Check at 4 hours!

8. Serve with brown gravy made from the au jus. Mix flour and cold water to make a thin paste in saucepan and gradually stir in the juice from the Crock-Pot. Delicious!

∽

MIXED BERRY CRUMBLE

Great for breakfast or desert! Spray a pretty glass pie plate with coconut oil.

1. Mix in one cup of sliced strawberries, one cup of blueberries, one cup of raspberries and one cup of blackberries.

2. Sprinkle about 1 tablespoon of sugar or honey and 1 tablespoon of cornstarch on top berries and mix well to kind of coat berries. Pour into glass pie dish.

3. For topping, melt one half of cup peanut or almond butter (I prefer almond butter) in microwave about 30 seconds.

4. Stir in 1 tablespoon coconut oil. Stir in one tablespoon of cinnamon. You can also

add a pinch of ginger.

5. Then mix in 1 cup of oats. You can also add preferred chopped nuts.

6. Coat the oats with the mixture. Sprinkle the oat topping on top of berries.

7. Bake at 375 degrees for 20 minutes and check on topping. If topping is crisp and brown, it is done.

8. Serve warm with your favorite vanilla ice cream.

✄

SAINT PATRICK'S DAY

"He found Ireland all heathen and left it all Christian."

–The World Book Encyclopedia (Chicago, IL: Field Enterprises, Inc., 1957, p. 6142)

Around 405 A.D., at the age of 16 years old, while working on his father's farm near the sea, 50 currachs (longboats) filled with raiders weaved their way toward the shore.

Mary Cagney, author of "Patrick The Saint" (*Christian History*, Issue 60), wrote:

> With no Roman army to protect them (Roman legions had long since deserted Britain to protect Rome from barbarian invasions), Patricius and his town were unprepared for attack.
>
> The Irish warriors, wearing helmets and armed with spears, descended on the pebble beach.
>
> The braying war horns struck terror into Patricius' heart, and he started to run toward town.

The warriors quickly demolished the village, and as Patricius darted among the burning houses and screaming women, he was caught. The barbarians dragged him aboard a boat bound for the east coast of Ireland.

For six years Patrick herded animals for a Druid chieftain. He later wrote in his life's story, called *The Confession of Saint Patrick:*

But after I came to Ireland – every day I had to tend sheep, and many times a day I prayed – the love of God and His fear came to me more and more, and my faith was strengthened.

And my spirit was moved so that in a single day I would say as many as a hundred prayers, and almost as many in the night, and this even when I was staying in the woods and on the mountains; and I used to get up for prayer before daylight, through snow, through frost, through rain ...

There the Lord opened the sense of my unbelief that I might at last remember my sins and be

> converted with all my heart to the
> Lord my God who ... comforted
> me as would a father his son.

Patrick returned to Ireland. He confronted the Druids, converted chieftains, and used the three–leaf clover to teach the Trinity.

The Druids tried to ambush and kill Patrick nearly a dozen times:

> Daily I expect murder, fraud
> or captivity, but I fear none of these
> things because of the promises of
> Heaven ...

> The merciful God often freed
> me from slavery and from twelve
> dangers in which my life was at
> stake – not to mention numerous
> plots ... God is my witness, who
> knows all things even before
> they come to pass, as He used
> to forewarn even me ... of many
> things by a divine message ...

> I came to the people of Ireland
> to preach the Gospel, and to suffer
> insult from the unbelievers ... I
> am prepared to give even my life
> without hesitation and most gladly
> for His name, and it is there that I
> wish to spend it until I die.

(Get the book, *Saint Patrick–The Real Story of His Amazing Life From Tragedy to Triumph.*)

My mother, Peggy Callahan, was the oldest of 13 children and always wore a "Kiss Me, I am Irish pin" and made this Irish meal on St. Patrick's Day!

❦

GRANDMA CALLAHAN'S CORNED BEEF

Grandma Peggy Callahan was the oldest of 13. She did not finish school because she had to take care of her siblings during the struggling years of the depression. She was an outstanding cook!

1. Place 1 rinsed and trimmed Corned Beef brisket in an oiled Dutch oven or large soup pot.

2. Add the juice from the brisket package.

3. Add 4 cups of water or enough to cover the beef.

4. Add 2 bay leaves, 1 teaspoon of whole cloves, 1 teaspoon caraway seeds, 1/2

teaspoon black pepper.

5. Bring to a boil. Lower the heat and simmer, covered for 2 ½ hours or until meat is tender.

6. Peel a strip around 6–8 small red potatoes and trim and slice 6 carrots. Add to Dutch oven.

7. Cut one large onion into 6 wedges and add to pot.

8. Add 1/2 small head cabbage also cut into wedges. You can also add 12 Brussels sprouts.

9. Bring to a boil. Lower heat and simmer for 15 minutes or until vegetables are tender.

10. Remove the corned beef brisket onto a platter and slice across the grain.

11. Arrange the vegetables around the meat and sprinkle with fresh chopped parsley.

❦

BEST ZUCCHINI BREAD–GREEN MUFFINS

The best Zucchini Bread recipe is also the best Green Muffin recipe.

1. Preheat oven to 350 degrees.

2. In a large bowl, mix together 3 cups of flour, 1 cup of sugar, 2 teaspoons of cinnamon, 1 teaspoon of salt, 1 teaspoon of baking powder, 1 teaspoon of baking soda.

3. In another bowl beat together 3 large eggs, 2 teaspoons of vanilla or 2 teaspoons almond extract (which I prefer) and 1 +1/3 cup Bertolli Light Olive Oil. The almond extract gives it a richer flavor and smells so good.

4. Pour over flour mixture and stir until mixed.

5. Mix in 3 cups shredded zucchini. You can add 1 cup chopped walnuts but I do not.

6. Pour batter into 12 greased individual bundtlettes or large muffin pans or small bread pans which will need to cook a little longer.

7. Bake for 30–35 minutes or until fork comes out clean.

∽

EASTER SUNDAY

"God moves in a mysterious way His wonders to perform ... Dear Bro. I know that my Redeemer liveth."

–George Washington Carver, writing to Rev. Lyman Ward, January 15, 1925:

Jesus, the "Lamb of God," was sacrificed on Jewish Feast of Passover; was in the grave on the Feast of Unleavened Bread; and was resurrected on Feast of First Fruits.

Passover was when each Israelite family in Egypt killed a lamb and put its blood over the doorposts of their house so that the angel of death would "pass over" during the final plague.

The Apostle Paul wrote:

For even Christ our passover is sacrificed for us. I Corinthians 5:7

The next day, the Israelites observed the Feast of Unleavened Bread, where they removed from their homes all the leaven or yeast, which was symbolic of sin. Providentially, the same day was when Jesus, "who taketh away the sins of the world," was in the tomb.

Paul wrote in I Corinthians 5:6–8:

> Let us keep the Feast, not with the old leaven, neither with the leaven of malice and wickedness; but with the unleavened bread of sincerity and truth.

On the third day, Israelites celebrated the Feast of First Fruits, when the first of the barley was harvested, as it was the first grain to ripen in the Land of Israel.

Jesus rose from the dead on the Feast of First Fruits. The Apostle Paul wrote

> But every man in his own order: Christ the first fruits; afterward they that are Christ's at his coming. I Corinthians 15:23

Sir Lionel Luckhoo, who is listed in the *Guinness Book of World Records* as world's most successful criminal attorney, stated:

> The bones of Muhammad are in Medina, the bones of Confucius are in Shantung, the cremated bones of Buddha are in Nepal. Thousands pay pilgrimages to worship at their tombs which contain their bones.

> But in Jerusalem there is a cave cut into the rock. This is the tomb of Jesus. IT IS EMPTY! YES, EMPTY! BECAUSE HE

IS RISEN! He died, physically and historically. He arose from the dead, and now sits at the right hand of God.

George Washington's tomb is engraved with John 11:25, where Jesus told Martha:

I am the Resurrection and the Life; sayeth the Lord. He that believeth in Me, though he were dead yet shall he live. And whosoever liveth and believeth in Me shall never die.

CARROT CAKE OR MUFFINS

When my children were little, I would make carrot cake in a lamb cake mold and talked to them about Jesus, the Lamb that was slain for our sins and rose from the Dead to open the Gates of Heaven for us.

You can also make it in 2 layers, cut each layer in 1/2 and make 2 bunny cakes like the one pictured here!

1. Preheat oven to 350 degrees.

2. Grate about 6 carrots to make 3 cups of grated carrots and set aside.

3. In large bowl, beat 1 ½ cup of oil (I use light olive oil for health benefits) 1 cup of brown sugar and 4 eggs, one at a time.

4. In another bowl mix together 2 cups of flour (I use unbleached white), 2 teaspoon of baking soda, 2 teaspoons of baking powder, 1/2 teaspoon of salt, and 2 teaspoons of cinnamon.

5. Blend the 2 mixtures together and then add the grated carrots and mix well.

6. If baking in 3 well–greased and floured cake pans, bake for 30 minutes or until fork comes out clean. If baking in a lamb shaped or 9 x 13–inch pan, bake 35 minutes or more if needed. Cupcakes or muffins will bake for about 20 minutes.

7. Top with Cream Cheese Frosting

Blend together 8 ounces of softened cream cheese (I use light) with 1/2 stick of softened butter, a little less than 1/4 cup milk, 1 pound of powdered sugar, 2 teaspoons of vanilla and frost when cake is cool.

8. I surround the sides with coconut. Some people also add 1/2 chopped pecans to the cake.

✥

CARROT APPLE SALAD

One of our favorites, this recipe will feed four people as a side salad. You can double it for more.

1. Chop 2 large red delicious apples into small bite size pieces.

2. Add 1/2 bag of grated carrots.

3. Squeeze the juice of one orange over this and grate a little zest on top.

4. I add about 1/3 cup of raisins and 1/4 cup of cashew pieces.

5. Stir in about 1 tablespoon of light mayonnaise or whip cream.

6. Top with about 1/4 cup pumpkin or sunflower seeds.

LEMON CHICKEN, GREEN BEANS & RED POTATOES

1. Preheat oven to 400 degrees.

2. Coat a large glass baking dish (9x13) or cast–iron skillet with 1 tablespoon of olive oil.

3. Arrange 2 thinly sliced lemons in a single layer on the bottom of the dish or skillet.

4. In a large bowl, combine 4 tablespoons of olive oil, the juice of one lemon, 1 teaspoon of salt and 3–4 cloves of fresh minced garlic with pepper to taste.

5. Add 4 bone in chicken breasts or thighs, 1/4 pound of trimmed green beans, and 8 small red potatoes quartered and toss to coat.

6. Arrange it all on top of the lemons. I sprinkle the top with a little paprika and some

fresh oregano leaves also.

7. Roast for 45 minutes or until cooked through. Serve warm.

❧

COCONUT MACAROONS

You can make little nests with jelly bean eggs in them for Easter.

1. In a medium bowl, combine 1 and 1/3 cup of sweetened shredded coconut, 1/3 cup of sugar, 2 tablespoons of flour, 1/8 teaspoon of salt.

2. Add 2 large egg whites beaten at room temperature with 1/2 teaspoon of vanilla

3. Drop by rounded teaspoonfuls onto greased baking sheets. I use coconut oil on the pans.

4. Bake at 325 degrees for about 18–20 minutes or until golden brown. Cool on a

wire rack.

    5. To make nests add about 1/3 teaspoon of green food coloring to the batter and when you take them out of the oven, place 3 small jellybeans into the middle while still warm.

    6. Another option is to dip the bottoms of them into 4 ounces of semisweet melted Ghirardelli or other fine chocolate before cooling on waxed paper!

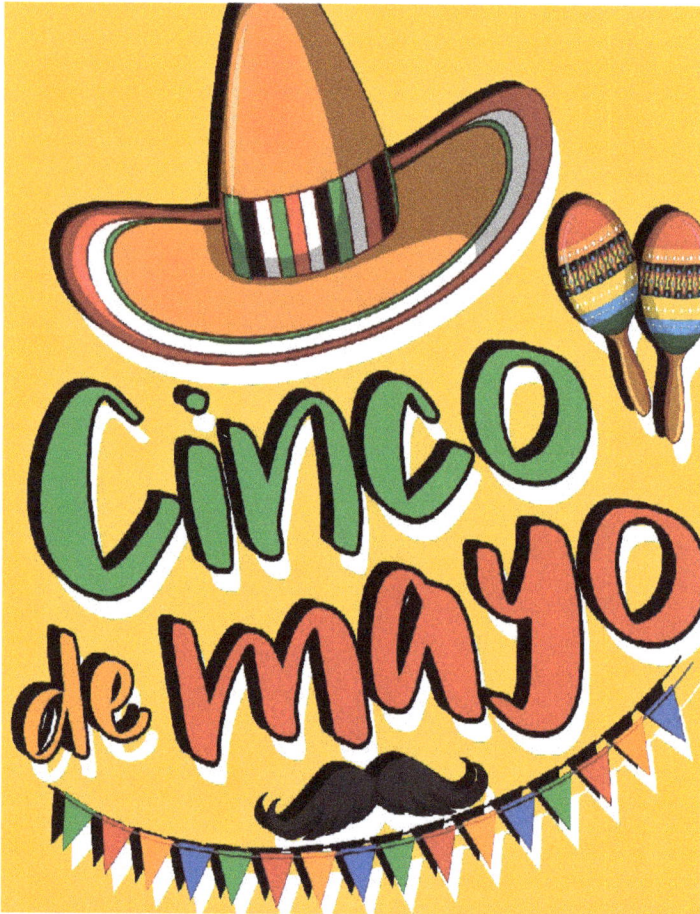

❧

CINCO DE MAYO

"Viva Mexico, viva la independencia!"–Last words of Maximilian I, June 19, 1867

Mexico had been part of the Spanish Empire since 1521 when Hernán Cortés conquered the Aztecs. In 1808, Napoleon invaded Spain, took King Fernando VII captive, and put his brother, Joseph Bonaparte, on the throne. Those in New Spain questioned if they should be loyal to this secular French king, especially since they were Catholic and Napoleon had been excommunicated by the Pope.

In 1808, Simon Bolivar began a revolt which led to the independence of Gran Columbia, namely Venezuela, Colombia (which included Panama), Ecuador, Peru, Bolivia, northern Peru, western Guyana, and northwest Brazil.

In 1810, a priest in Mexico named Miguel Hidalgo gave a sermon "The Cry of Dolores (Sorrows)," He put the image of the Virgin of Guadalupe on a banner and rallied 90,000 peasant farmers. His ill-equipped followers inscribed slogans on their flags: "Long live religion! Long live our most Holy Mother of Guadalupe! Long live America and death to bad government!" Though Hidalgo was captured and executed, he is considered the "Father of the Nation of Mexico."

From 1810 to 1820, General Agustín de Iturbide fought for the Spanish Monarchy against Hidalgo's revolutionaries, but then he switched to fight against Spain. On September 27 1821, Mexico became officially independent from Spain, but instead of setting up a constitutional republic like the United States, Iturbide made himself Emperor. He followed Napoleon's example of placing the crown on his own head in 1822.

Antonio López de Santa Anna and others conspired against Iturbie and he fled to Britain. Upon return, Iturbide was executed. In 1824, Guadalupe Victoria was elected as the first President—the only President for the next 30 years to complete his full term. The pattern was that those who usurped power would set up committees to do investigations to root out and destroy previous Presidents and supporters to prevent their reelection.

From 1821 to 1857, Mexico had 50 different governments. This was called the Age of Santa Anna, as he ruled as President for 12 non-consecutive terms, then laid aside the Constitution and ruled as dictator.

In 1854, Benito Juárez began the Revolution of Ayutla, forcing Santa Anna to resign. In 1856, Juárez, backed by Freemasons, led a War of Reform against the Catholic Church, confiscating church property and suppressing religious orders. Once President, Juárez stopped paying interest on Mexico's debt to Spain, Britain and France in 1861. This provoked those nations to plan an invasion.

While the United States occupied in the Civil War, French troops landed in 1862, supported by various Mexican financial and church leaders. The French troops suffered a minor setback on May 5, 1862 – "Cinco de Mayo" – with a defeat at the Battle of Puebla. It is speculated that had the French not suffered this setback, they may have taken Mexico sooner and been in a position to alter the America Civil War by supplying arms to the Confederates.

The French army regrouped and captured Mexico City, Guadalajara, Zacatecas. Acapulco, Durango, Sinaloa and Jalisco. Many Mexican leaders traveled to Europe to plead with Maximilian I to come to Mexico and restore order. He agreed, arriving at Veracruz to joyful crowds on May 21, 1864.

Maximilian created an avenue through the center of Mexico City known as the boulevard Paseo de la Reforma. His wife, Carlota, was shocked by the living conditions of the lower classes and raised money from wealthy Mexicans to help supply poor houses.

Maximilian abolished child labor and reduced working hours for laborers. He canceled all debts for peasants over 10 pesos, restored communal property and broke the monopoly of Hacienda stores. He forbade all forms of corporal punishment and decreed that poor people could no longer be bought and sold for the price of their debt.

To the dismay of the wealthy, Maximilian upheld liberal policies of land reforms, religious freedom, and extended the right to vote beyond the landholding class.

The U.S. did not want any European powers to have a presence in the Western Hemisphere, as stated in the Monroe Doctrine, so U.S. diplomats pressured Napoleon III to abandon Maximilian.

Lincoln supported Benito Juárez, with the U.S. secretly "losing" arms and ammunition at El Paso del Norte near the Mexican border. General Philip Sheridan wrote: "We continued supplying arms and munitions to the liberals, sending as many as 30,000 muskets from Baton Rouge alone."

In 1867, France finally withdrew its army. Though there were later revolutions, Cinco de Mayo is the day chosen to celebrate Mexico's Independence!

❧

TORTILLA SOUP

This recipe makes a big pot serving at least six

1. Preheat oven to 450 degrees.

2. Oil a sheet pan with olive oil and roast 2 yellow onions sliced, 2 cloves of garlic, and 1 or 2 large diced red tomatoes 15 to 20 minutes.

3. In a large stockpot heat 1/4 cup of olive oil and fry 8 corn tortillas cut in strips and set aside on paper towels. Then fry 5 Ancho chiles seeded and sliced into strips in the oil.

Add the other roasted vegetables with 2 tablespoons of cumin, 1 tablespoon of coriander, salt and pepper to taste.

4. Deglaze the stockpot with 8 ounce of tomato juice or V–8.

5. Add 8 cups of chicken broth and bring to a boil. Reduce heat and simmer vegetables and chiles for 40 minutes.

6. Let it cool a little while grilling 3 chicken breasts on a grill pan or outside grill and chop into bite size pieces.

7. Add 1 bunch of cilantro, with stems removed, to the soup base and blend with immersion blender or food processor until smooth.

8. Add kernels from 2 cooked cobbs of corn or 1 can drained corn and season to taste with salt, pepper and the juice of 1 lime.

9. Serve in 8 ounce bowls topped with

grated white cheddar or Mexican blend shredded cheese and the tortilla strips you made earlier. You can also garnish with a sprig of cilantro.

❧

EASY CHICKEN & SPINACH ENCHILADAS

My kids loved these!

1. Spray 14 x 9 x 2 or 3–inch glass baking sheet with avocado or olive oil.

2. Line the dish with 5 small corn tortillas. I cut the last one in half to cover the bottom of the pan perfectly.

3. Mix together 2 cups of chopped boiled or grilled chicken and one can cream of chicken soup (you can use healthy low–fat soup) Stir in 2 tablespoons of fire roasted salsa or your favorite salsa and 1 cup of grated Colby Jack or Mexican blend shredded cheese.

4. Cover the 5 tortillas with the chicken mixture and top with 1/2 bag chopped fresh

spinach or 1 box drained defrosted frozen spinach. Top with a little more grated cheese and 5 more corn tortillas.

5. I pour 1 can Old El Paso Enchilada sauce over the tortillas. This is best but you can use a jar of your favorite salsa as long as it is thick.

6. Cover with more shredded cheese and bake at 400 degrees for 25–30 minutes until cheese is a little browned.

7. I top each slice with a little grated lettuce, a scoop of guacamole and a little chopped tomato.

IRENE'S YUM YUM CAKE

This is the Best Chocolate Cinnamon cake ever! We made it for birthdays and even in little loaf pans for Christmas gifts.

1. Mix 2 cups of flour and 2 cups of sugar in large bowl.

2. Put 1 stick of butter, 1 cup of water, 1/2 cup of butter flavor Crisco in large pot and bring to a boil.

3. Stir in 3 ½ tablespoons cocoa and 1 teaspoon of cinnamon (I use a little more).

4. Pour the flour and sugar mixture into

the pot. Mix well and let cool for about 10 minutes.

5. Pour in 1/2 cup of buttermilk and mix, then blend in 2 beaten eggs, and a teaspoon of baking soda.

6. Blend well and pour into about 3 greased loaf pans or 5 little loaf pans or one 14x9 inch glass baking dish.

7. Bake at 375 for 30 minutes or until done depending on size of pans.

8. Melt one stick of butter and boil with 1/3 cup of milk and 3 ½ tablespoons of cocoa.

9. Gradually beat in one box of powdered sugar and pour warm icing over hot cakes.

10. Let icing cool before serving.

Happy Mother's Day Mom!-

You are the best and most beautiful mom in the whole world. Thank you so much for everything you do and all the delicious meals you cook! You're the best!

Love Mike

❧
MOTHER'S DAY

"**A**ll that I am, or hope

to be, I owe to my angel mother!"

– Abraham Lincoln

A Mother's Day celebration was held in Boston in 1872 at the suggestion of abolitionist and suffragist Julia Ward Howe, writer of "The Battle Hymn of the Republic."

In the following decades, numerous Mother's Day efforts sprang up.

One was in 1904, by the administrator of the University of Notre Dame, Frank Hering, After observing students sending penny postcards to their mothers, he proposed "setting aside one day in the year as a nationwide memorial to the memories of mothers and motherhood," writing:

> Throughout history the great men of the world have given their credit for their achievements to their mothers. The Holy Church recognizes this.

The person who successfully made Mother's Day into a national event was

Anna Jarvis, of Grafton, West Virginia, the granddaughter of a Baptist minister.

Anna Jarvis was a member of Andrews Methodist Episcopal Church, where she taught Sunday school.

In 1876, after one of her lessons, she closed with a prayer:

> I hope and pray that someone, sometime, will found a memorial mother's day commemorating her for the matchless service she renders to humanity in every field of life. She is entitled to it.

Anna Jarvis' mother, during the Civil War, had organized Mothers' Day Work Clubs to care for wounded soldiers, both Union and Confederate.

Anna's mother raised money for medicine, inspected bottled milk, improved sanitation and hired women to care for families where mothers suffered from tuberculosis, May 9, 1905.

Inspired by her mother's self–sacrifice and generosity, Anna Jarvis wanted to honor her and all mothers.

On May 12, 1907, Anna persuaded her church, Andrews Methodist Episcopal Church, to have a small Mother's Day service.

The church then agreed to set aside every year the 2nd Sunday in May, the anniversary of her mother's death, as a day to show appreciation to all mothers – the makers of the home.

The next year, May 10, 1908, Anna organized a Mother's Day event in two places: Andrews Methodist Episcopal Church, where she sent a telegram; and in Philadelphia, where she gave a moving speech in the auditorium of the 12–story Wanamaker Department Store.

John Wanamaker was a retail pioneer and founder of one the first department stores. Wanamaker, who had paintings of Christ throughout his store, stated:

> There is a power in the Gospel of the Lord Jesus Christ. Keep uppermost the profound conviction that it is the Gospel that is to win the heart and convert the world.

With the financial backing of John Wanamaker and H.J. Heinz, maker of "57 varieties," Anna Jarvis began a letter–writing campaign to ministers and politicians to establish a "national" Mothers' Day.

Due to the overwhelming support of pastors and churches, by 1909, forty–five states observed Mother's Day.

People wore white and red Carnations on Sunday to pay tribute to their mothers.

On May 9, 1914, President Woodrow Wilson proclaimed the first National Mothers' Day as a: "public expression of ... love and reverence for the mothers of our country."

❦

JESSICA'S BANANA BREAD

My daughter makes the best!

1. Preheat oven to 350 degrees.

2. Smash 3 or 4 ripe bananas in large mixing bowl.

3. Mix in 1/3 cup of melted butter with a wooden spoon.

4. Add 3/4 cup of sugar, 1 teaspoon of vanilla, 1 beaten egg and 1 teaspoon of baking soda and a pinch of salt

5. Stir in 1 ½ cups flour (Whole wheat or all–purpose can be used)

6. Pour mixture into 2 greased 4 x8 inch loaf pans

7. We top with chocolate chips, nuts, blueberries or streusel.

8. Bake for 45 minutes and cool before serving.

❧

LAYERED GARDEN SALAD

Serve this in a large punch bowl. It is lovely for a gathering!

1. Thaw one box of frozen peas and place in bottom of punch bowl.

2. Place on small bag grated carrots on top of that.

3. Next 1 small cucumber or 1/2 large chopped.

4. 1–2 cuts of grated colby jack cheese or whatever cheese you prefer.

5. 3 cups of chopped romaine lettuce..

6. 1 small bag baby spinach.

7. Make a dressing out of 1 ½ cup mayonnaise. (I use Hellmann's Light), 1 tablespoon of sugar, 2 teaspoons of lemon

pepper, 1/4 cup of grated Parmesan for dressing and spread it over the top. You can also use a thick ranch dressing.

8. Top with 3 strips of cooked crumbled bacon or turkey bacon and surround the top of the bowl with little cherry tomatoes.

9. Take to dinner layered, and mix before the guests! Beautiful!!!

❧

LEMON CHICKEN SOUP

1. Boil 4 chicken breasts in sea salted water for 20–30 minutes and set on a plate to cool, but save the broth in the pot.

2. In saucepan, sauté 1/2 yellow sweet onion, 2 cloves of garlic, 3–4 stalks of chopped celery, and 2 –3 large chopped carrots in olive oil until softened. I chop everything pretty small.

3. Add this to your broth with fresh chopped parsley, oregano and fresh basil

to taste, (I use about 2 tablespoons of each) add pepper to taste and simmer for about 30 minutes. Add 1 ½ cup of orzo and simmer 10 minutes. Chop the chicken breast into bite size pieces and add to soup. Sometimes I also add peas.

4. Take seed out of 2 lemons and squeeze one lemon into the soup.

5. Serve a lemon wedge on the side of the bowl.

❧

CHICKEN DIVAN

Actually one of Bill's favorites, but lovely for a special dinner for a new Mommy

1. Boil 4–5 chicken breasts or whole chicken for 25 minutes in boiling salted water until done.

2. Cool on a plate.

3. Boil 1 ½ cup of rice in 3 cups of water

for 20 minutes or according to directions. You can use brown or wild rice, but we use white Jasmine.

4. Also boil a bag of chopped broccoli in separate pot or use the microwave steamers–2 bags.

5. Lightly oil the bottom and sides of a 14 x 9x 2–inch glass baking dish.

6. Layer the rice on the bottom of the baking dish

7. Next layer the chicken after chopping into bite size pieces

8. Drain the broccoli and layer on top of chicken.

9. Mix 1 can cream of chicken soup and 1/2 cup mayonnaise and spread on top of broccoli.

10. Top with grated cheddar or Colby Jack Cheese.

11. Bake at 375 degrees for about 30 minutes or until cheese is a little browned.

12. Boiled carrots with a squeeze of orange is a lovely side for this dish, or applesauce is delicious too.

~∽~

EASY CHOCOLATE MOUSSE

1. In a small saucepan, sprinkle 1 envelope of unflavored gelatin in ¼ cup cold water and let stand 1 minute.

2. Stir mixture over low heat about 3 minutes until gelatin dissolves completely.

3. In a blender or food processor, whirl together 1 ¼ cup of skim milk, 1/2 cup of sugar, 1/3 cup of cocoa powder, and 1 teaspoon of vanilla until blended.

4. While still processing, gradually add gelatin mixture through feed cap, whirling until blended.

5. Pour mixture into medium bowl and using a wire whisk blend in 1 ½ cups of

whipped topping.

    6. Pour into pretty dessert or sundae dishes and refrigerate about 2 hours until set.

    7. Top with whipped topping and other garnishes such as fresh raspberries as desired.

❧
MEMORIAL DAY

"Here rests in honored glory an American soldier known but to God."

—Inscription on Tomb of the Unknown Soldier, Arlington Cemetery

General Douglas MacArthur told West Point cadets, May 1962:

The soldier, above all other men, is required to practice the greatest act of religious training– sacrifice. In battle and in the face of danger and death, he discloses those Divine attributes which his Maker gave when He created man in His own image ...

No physical courage and no brute instinct can take the place of Divine help which alone can sustain him.

However horrible the incidents of war may be, the soldier who is called upon to offer and to give his life for his country is the noblest development of mankind.

Memorial Day in America began during the Civil War when southern women scattered spring flowers on graves of both northern Union and southern Confederate soldiers, Memorial Day grew to honor all who gave their lives defending America's freedom in every war, including:

- Revolutionary War: 1775–83 – 25,000;

- War of 1812: – 20,000;

- Mexican–American War: 1846–48 – 13,283;

- Civil War: 1861–65 – 625,000;

- Spanish–American War: 1898 – 2,446;

- World War 1: 1917–18 – 116,516;

- World War 2: 1941–45 – 405,399;

- Korean War: 1950–53 – 36,516;

- Vietnam War: 1955–75 – 58,209;

- Persian Gulf War: 1990–91 – 258;

- Operation Enduring Freedom (Afghanistan): 2001–14 – 2,356;

- Operation Iraqi Freedom: 2003–12 – 4,489;

- Ongoing wars against Islamic terrorism.

In 1968, one hundred years after the first observance, Memorial Day was moved to the last Monday in May.

⁂

BARBEQUE BEEF BRISKET

This is great for a Party but start 2 days before!

1. Place 5–6 pound brisket on a large sheet of heavy–duty foil.

2. Sprinkle both sides of the meat with liquid smoke and onion salt, celery salt and garlic salt and pepper to taste. Seal the foil and refrigerate overnight.

3. To bake, place foil wrapped brisket in a baking dish and bake at 300 degrees for 5–6 hours.

4. Transfer brisket to a clean piece of heavy–duty foil and refrigerate for several hours.

5. Take the foil off and place brisket in the baking dish without it.

6. Slice brisket across the grain and cover with your favorite Barbeque sauce.

7. Reheat 30–40 minutes at 325 degrees and serve warm.

❧

GRANDMA PEGGY'S COLESLAW

1. In a large pretty bowl, place 1/2 head of cabbage chopped into thin small ribbons (about 2 cups)

2. Add 1/4 cup chopped fine red cabbage and 1/4 cup shredded carrots. (I add more carrots)

3. Cover with 1/4 to 1/3 cups of Marzetti slaw dressing. It is the best, but you can also use sweet onion or poppyseed dressing if you like.

4. Sprinkle a little paprika on top and

black pepper if you prefer.

5. I line the bowl around the outside with sliced tomatoes and cucumbers.

6. To give it a tropical twist you can also add finely diced pineapple.

7. In the fall, I add finely chopped red delicious apple.

~❧~

TWICE BAKED POTATOES

These are perfect to warm up with the brisket and can be made ahead of time.

1.Cut baked potatoes in half lengthwise while still warm and scoop out the inside keeping the peel intact like a little boat.

2. Measurements depend on how many potatoes you are making. Mix warm potato with as much butter and or sour cream as you desire and a little milk to make the mashed potato consistency

3. Season with salt, pepper, paprika, chives, and fill the potato shells with the mashed potatoes.

4. Top with your favorite cheese like Colby Jack or cheddar, and chopped bacon if you like.

5. Bake at 325 degrees for 30 minutes with the brisket.

RED, WHITE & BLUE JELL–O SWIRL CAKE

1. Bake a white cake mix in a 14x 9–inch baking dish according to directions.

2. Take the cake out of the oven and while it is cooling for 5 minutes, make a small package of raspberry or strawberry Jell–O using 1 cup of ice–cold water at the end and mix well.

3. Poke holes in the cake with a large serving fork or the round end of a chopstick and gently pour Jell–O over the top of the

cake to fill the holes and make pretty swirls in the cake.

4. Refrigerate cake for about 4 hours and then top with cool whip or homemade whipped cream. You can also make a layer of vanilla instant pudding and then top that with cool whip.

5. I make it look like a flag with blueberries in the corner for the star section and stripe the rest of the cake with slide strawberries and or raspberries. Refrigerate until it is all enjoyed!

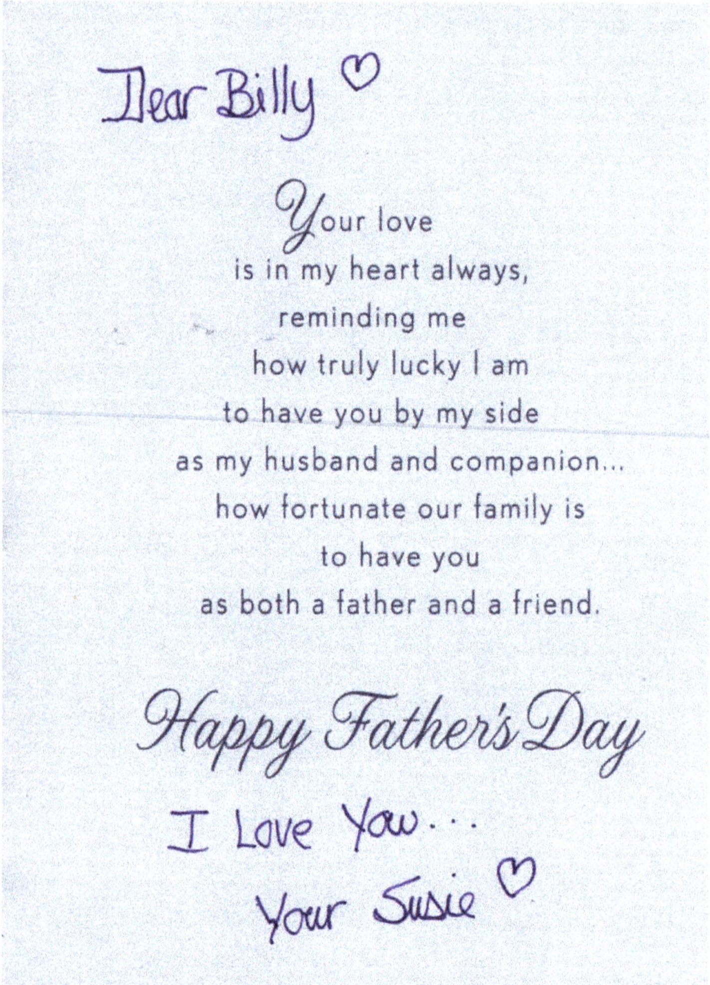

Dear Billy ♡

Your love
is in my heart always,
reminding me
how truly lucky I am
to have you by my side
as my husband and companion...
how fortunate our family is
to have you
as both a father and a friend.

Happy Father's Day

I Love You...
Your Susie ♡

༄

FATHER'S DAY

"The call today is for Christian heroes"

– U.S. Senate Chaplain Peter Marshall

The first formal "Father's Day" was celebrated JUNE 19, 1910, in Spokane, Washington.

Sonora Louise Smart Dodd heard a church sermon on the newly established Mother's Day and wanted to honor her father, Civil War veteran William Jackson Smart, who had raised six children by himself after his wife died in childbirth.

Sonora Louise Smart Dodd drew up a petition supported by the Young Men's Christian Association and the ministers of Spokane to celebrate Fathers' Day.

In 1916, Woodrow Wilson spoke at a Spokane Fathers' Day service.

On December 6, 1904, President Theodore Roosevelt addressed Congress:

> No Christian and civilized
> community can afford to show
> a happy–go–lucky lack of
> concern for the youth of today;
> for, if so, the community will

have to pay a terrible penalty of financial burden and social degradation in the tomorrow.

On Father's Day, 1988, Ronald Reagan said:

Children, vulnerable and dependent, desperately need security, and it has ever been a duty and a joy of fatherhood to offer it.

Being a father requires strength ... and more than a little courage ... to persevere, to fight discouragement, and to keep working for the family ...

Reagan ended:

Let us ... express our thanks and affection to our fathers, whether we can do so in person or in prayer.

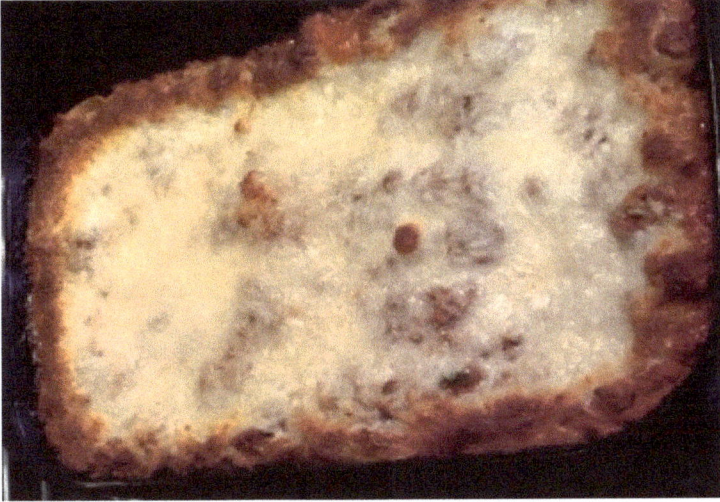

LASAGNA

Our family's favorite Lasagna (can be made the day before and just baked on the holiday)

1. Oil a 14x9 inch baking dish and line with no boil lasagna noodles.

2. Make a sauce by browning 1 pound of Italian sausage a little and then add 1 pound lean ground beef to finish cooking until almost done. Drain the fat. I also add 1–2 cloves of chopped garlic and about 1/2 chopped sweet onion while browning. Then add fresh chopped basil and oregano and one 6 ounce can of tomato paste and one jar of Classico Tomato Basil Sauce or your favorite homemade or jarred sauce and simmer.

3. Make the cheese filling out of 1 ½ cup part skim ricotta cheese, 1/3 cup grated Parmesan, 1 egg, 1/4 cup of minced parsley

blended well. Put 1/2 of the cheese filling on the noodles in the pan.

4. Ladle 1/2 of the sauce over the ricotta and sprinkle grated Parmesan or Italian mix cheese on top of the sauce.

5. Repeat the layers but put extra grated cheese on the very top.

6. Bake uncovered in 375 degrees oven for 40 minute and check. You will know when it is done because the cheese will be a little browned.

❧

ZUCCHINI STICKS

You can bake these in the oven with the Lasagna and after 25 minutes enjoy as an appetizer. Save a little sauce to dip them in!

1. Rinse 2 medium zucchini and trim off the ends. Don't peel them.

2. Cut in half and then cut in half lengthwise and finally into 1/2 inch sticks. You should end up with about 16 pieces.

3. Put 1/3 cup of flour in one bowl. Whisk

2 eggs with 1 tablespoon of milk in another bowl, and in a 3rd bowl, combine 1 cup Panko or breadcrumbs with 1/2 Parmesan cheese and 1 teaspoon fresh minced oregano, 1/2 teaspoon paprika and salt and pepper to taste.

4. Coat each zucchini stick lightly with flour, then dip in the egg wash and finally roll in the Panko mixture.

5. Place the zucchini sticks on a parchment–lined baking sheet and bake for 20 minutes at 375 degrees. They should be crispy if done!

6. Remove from the oven and serve warm with your favorite sauce.

❧

COLOSSAL COOKIES

This is perfect for Father's Day! These are great flourless cookies!

1. Heat oven to 350 degrees.

2. In a very large bowl, beat together 1/2 cup of butter softened to room temperature,

18 ounces of chunky peanut butter, with 1 cup firmly packed brown sugar or 1 cup of honey, 4 eggs and 1 teaspoon of vanilla and 2 ½ teaspoon baking soda.

Then mix in 1 tablespoon of cinnamon and I add 1 teaspoon ginger.

3. Stir in 6 cups of quick or old–fashioned oats, one 6 ounce package semisweet chocolate chips, and raisins or chopped dates if you prefer.

4. Drop about 1 tablespoon of dough rolled into a ball and flattened just a little or use large cookie scoop to place about 12 cookies on an ungreased cookie sheet.

5. Bake 10–12 minutes. Cool one minute on cookie sheet and remove to cool on wire rack or on parchment paper.

Store tightly covered. Dough can be frozen and when ready to bake, let stand at room temperature about 30 minutes before shaping cookies.

❧

INDEPENDENCE DAY

"In this country of ours took place THE GREATEST REVOLUTION that has ever taken place IN THE WORLD'S HISTORY—Every other revolution simply exchanged one set of rulers for another ...

Here for THE FIRST TIME in all the THOUSANDS OF YEARS of man's relation to man ... the founding fathers established the idea that you and I had within ourselves the GOD–GIVEN RIGHT AND ABILITY to DETERMINE OUR OWN DESTINY."

–Ronald Reagan, 1961

The Declaration of Independence, signed July 4, 1776, listed 27 reasons why Americans declared their independence from 38–year–old King George III:

He has made judges dependent on his will alone ...

He has erected a multitude of new offices, and sent hither swarms of officers to harass our people and eat out their substance ... He has kept among us, in times of peace, standing armies ... To subject us to a jurisdiction foreign to our constitution ...

For quartering large bodies of armed troops among us ... For imposing taxes on us without our consent ...

For depriving us in many cases, of the benefit of trial by jury ... For ... establishing ... an arbitrary government ... For ... altering fundamentally the forms of our governments ...

He has plundered our seas, ravaged our coasts, burnt our towns, and destroyed the lives of our people.

He is at this time transporting large armies of foreign mercenaries to complete the works of death, desolation, and tyranny ...

He has excited domestic insurrections amongst us,

John Hancock, the 39–year–old President of the Continental Congress, signed the Declaration first, reportedly saying "the price on my head has just doubled."

Many of the 56 signers sacrificed their prosperity for their posterity:

- 11 had their homes destroyed,
- 5 were hunted and captured,
- 17 served in the military, and
- 9 died during the war.

Signers were as young as 27–years–old and as old as 70–year–old Ben Franklin, who remarked:

> We must hang together or most
> assuredly we shall hang separately.

Thirty–three year–old Thomas Jefferson's original rough draft of the Declaration contained a line condemning slavery, as the King of England was part owner of the Royal African Company:

> He has waged cruel war against human nature itself ... in the persons of a distant people who never offended him, captivating and carrying them into slavery in another hemisphere, or to incur miserable death in their transportation thither ... suppressing every legislative attempt to prohibit or to restrain this execrable commerce determining to keep open a market where MEN should be bought and sold.

The Declaration referred to God:

> Laws of Nature and of NATURE'S GOD ...

> All Men are created equal, that they are endowed by their CREATOR with certain unalienable Rights ..

> Appealing to the SUPREME JUDGE OF THE WORLD for the rectitude of our intentions ...

> And for the support of this Declaration, with a firm reliance on the protection of DIVINE PROVIDENCE, we mutually pledge to each other our Lives, our Fortunes, and our sacred Honor.

This was revolutionary, as kings did not believe everyone was created equal. They believed kings were created extra special. It was called "the divine right of kings," namely, that the Creator gave rights to the king, who dispensed them at his discretion to his lowly subjects.

The Declaration of Independence bypassed the King by declaring that the Creator gives rights directly to each citizen.

Forty–one year–old John Adams wrote to his wife of the Declaration:

> I am apt to believe that it will

be celebrated, by succeeding generations, as the great anniversary Festival. It ought to be commemorated, as the Day of Deliverance by SOLEMN ACTS OF DEVOTION TO GOD ALMIGHTY.

It ought to be solemnized with pomp and parade, with shows, games, sports, guns, bells, bonfires and illuminations from one End of this Continent to the other from this time forward forever more.

❧

STRAWBERRY, BLUEBERRY CREPES
1. In a medium size mixing bowl, crack 4 large eggs and whisk with about 1/4 cup

of milk.

2. Whisk in 1/2 teaspoon of vanilla and 1/4 cup of heart healthy Bisquick.

3. Spray a skillet with coconut oil spray and warm on high.

4. Pour about 1/4 of the batter into the hot greased skillet and swirl so crepe batter covers the bottom evenly and cook until edges start to brown.

5. Put 1st crepe on a plate and keep warm in the oven until you repeat and have 4 crepes.

6. Sprinkle the top crepe with a little cinnamon and fill with sliced strawberries, raspberries and or blueberries. My daughter likes to also put some Greek yogurt in the center.

7. Roll and top with whipped cream. Repeat with each crepe!

8. You can also fill them with chopped cooked bacon, spinach, and cheese for a savory alternative. Tomatoes, onions and cheese also make a nice filling.

❦

CROCK-POT CHILI

1. Grease the bottom of the inside of the Crock-Pot with a little olive oil.

2. Place 1–2 pounds of ground beef or turkey crumbled in the Crock-Pot depending upon how meaty you want it.

3. Saute 1/2 yellow onion, 1 clove of garlic, 1/2 cup of finely diced celery and 1/2 cup of finely chopped carrots, and 1/3 cup of assorted chopped peppers according to your heat tolerance in a little olive oil until tender.

4. Pour sautéed veggies on top of the meat in the Crock-Pot.

5. Add 1 can of chili beans and 1 can of tomato puree (sauce will also do)

6. Season with about 1 tablespoon chili powder, 1–2 teaspoon of cumin and turmeric, salt and pepper to taste.

7. Turn Crock-Pot on high and stir every 2 hours, cooking for about 4 hours or until meat is done.

8. If you are working an 8–hour day, just cook the chili on low.

❧

SEVEN LAYER MEXICAN DIP

This goes great with the chili.

1. In a large glass bowl, layer 1 can of fat free refried beans.

2. Top that with guacamole.

3. Next a layer of chopped tomatoes.

4. Top with a small layer of light sour cream.

5. Next sprinkle on a lot of grated

Mexican, Colby Jack or cheddar cheese blend

6. Top with chopped black olives and sliced jalapeños

7. Enjoy with chips. We like Blue corn tortilla chips with it.

❦

MIKE'S KRISPIE COOKIES

This is our son Mike's favorite!

Prepare a 13x9–inch pan with a little coconut oil spray and pour about 4 cups of Rice Krispies into baking dish. Top with about 1/4 bag of butterscotch chips.

1. Place 1/2 stick of butter in a Pyrex round casserole dish that is microwave safe

2. Add 1/3 cup of Peanut Butter and microwave 1 minute

3. Stir in 1 bag of fresh miniature marshmallows and microwave 1 more minute

4. Stir and make sure marshmallows are melting. Microwave 30 seconds more to makes sure mixture is melted together

5. Pour melted mixture over the Rice Krispies and mix quickly before it gets too sticky.

6. I always add about 1/2 cup more Rice Krispies and top with scattered chocolate chips or M&Ms

7. Press the cookies down and together with a sheet of waxed paper.

8. Cool and store covered with Saran Wrap.

✂ LABOR DAY

"God saw all that He had made, and it was very good. And there was evening, and there was morning—the sixth day ... Thus the heavens and the earth were finished ... And God blessed the seventh day, and sanctified it: because that in it He had rested from all his work which God created and made."

– Genesis 1:31; 2:3

To appreciate Labor Day, one needs to know the history preceding it. At the time the United States was founded, most people were farmers or worked in trades, such as:

apothecary, baker, blacksmith, butcher, cabinetmaker, carpenter, chandler (candlemaker), cobbler (shoemaker), cooper (barrelmaker), gunsmith, milliner (clothes merchant), printer, tailor, upholsterer, wheelwright (wheel craftsman).

The Industrial Revolution began in the late 18th century. Coal mines in Britain kept filling up with water. Scottish inventor James Watt came up with an invention to pump water out – a steam pump.

Steam was soon harnessed in the early 19th century to not just power pumps, but railroad steam engines, steam boats, and textile manufacturing machines.

This led to the creation of factories which mass produced items inexpensively. European manufactured products were imported into America.

Soon, Americans built factories. Inventions and advances in manufacturing made more goods available at cheaper prices. This resulted in Americans experiencing the fastest increase in the standard of living of any people in world history.

Factories had a continual source of workers from the millions of immigrants, who not only got a job, but learned the language and trade skills.

In May of 1886, a peaceful protest in Chicago near the McCormick Harvesting Machine Company plant turned into the Haymarket Riot. A peaceful protester threw dynamite at the police. The blast and subsequent violence killed seven police officers, four civilians, and wounded dozens.

To commemorate the incident, they chose May 1st. President Grover Cleveland thought it might improve his chances of getting re-elected in 1894 if he appeased workers with a national "LABOR DAY."

He intentionally did not choose May 1st as it was the anniversary of the bloody Chicago's Haymarket Riot and the "International Workers Day." He instead chose the FIRST MONDAY in SEPTEMBER.

Laborers worked hard for wages with which they bought houses, cars, trucks, boats, guns, and other personal possessions. The Bible calls this being "blessed."

They could voluntarily give away some of their possessions to those in need. The Bible calls this "charity."

In socialist countries, labors were forced to work hard, but could own no possessions. The government took them all away. People with no possessions have nothing with which to be charitable.

Socialists believe that when the government finally takes away everyone's possessions throughout the whole world, then an ideal utopia will appear called "communism."

The term "communism" comes from the Latin word "communis," meaning everything "held in common." There will be no private ownership of anything, no privacy, not even control over their own children. The government will control everything from production to consumption.

In 1971, John Lennon and his second wife, Yoko Ono, co–wrote the song "Imagine," with socialist–themed lyrics: "Imagine no possessions ... And no religion too."

Alexander Solzhenitsyn spent 11 years in labor camps of Union of Soviet Socialist

Republics. He warned American workers of the hidden danger of "social justice" movements, June 30, 1975:

> I ... call upon America to be more careful with its trust ...

> Prevent those ... who are attempting to establish even finer ... legal shades of equality – because of their distorted outlook ... short–sightedness and ... self–interest – from falsely using the struggle for peace and for social justice to lead you down a false road ...

> They are trying to weaken you; they are trying to disarm your strong and magnificent country in the face of this fearful threat ... I call upon you: ordinary working men of America ... do not let yourselves become weak.

(Get the book *SOCIALISM–The Real History from Plato to the Present: How the Deep State Capitalizes on Crises to Consolidate Control*)

I think of Labor Day as the last holiday of summer with a trip to the beach before it gets cold so let's serve grilled fish!

DEDE'S TUNA SALAD

My husband's grandmother would always make this when we visited her in Neosho, Missouri.

1. Drain 2 cans of tuna in water. (I prefer StarKist chunk light.) Put in a medium sized mixing bowl.

2. Peel and finely chop 2 hard boiled eggs and add to tuna.

3. I add 3 tablespoons of light Mayonnaise. You can add more if you like.

4. Add 2–3 tablespoons of sweet pickle relish to taste.

5. Mix all these ingredients together and then add 1/3–1/2 cup of finely chopped celery.

6. Dede always added some fresh chives and chopped green olives!

7. Top with a little black pepper.

8. Serve on a bed of chopped lettuce or

on toast with a sliced fresh tomato.

9. You can also make about a cup of bow tie or shellroni pasta and add it to the tuna. It makes a nice meal topped with some halved cherry tomatoes or cooked fresh green peas.

✍

GRILLED MAHI WITH PINEAPPLE SALSA

1. In a medium size glass bowl mix 2 cups of diced fresh pineapple. (You can also use canned tidbits)

2. Add 1/2 cup of diced onions, 1/2 cup of diced cherry tomatoes and chopped jalapeno to taste and the juice of 1/2 fresh lime. Set aside.

3. Heat a little olive oil on bottom of a grill pan. When oil is warm, place 4 Mahi filets on the grill pan and cook about 5 minutes on

each side until done. You can grill some fresh asparagus and or zucchini with the fish.

4. Squeeze the other 1/2 of the lime over the fish and salt and pepper to taste. I also sprinkle a little paprika on them.

5. Place a filet on each plate and top with a big spoon of pineapple salsa. Asparagus on the side.

6. We serve it with a Caribbean rice on the side. Guacamole and chips are great with it also.

❧

CINNAMON APPLE PIE À LA MODE

My grandmother said to use Pillsbury refrigerated pie crusts after making pies all of her life, so roll out one of the crusts into a glass pie dish.

1. Peel and chop 5 or six large apples of your choice into bite size smiles and place in glass bowl.

2. Stir in about 1/2 cup of sugar, 1–2 tablespoons of flour and about 1 tablespoon of cinnamon or adjust to your taste. We love cinnamon. Add a pinch of salt. You can also add a pinch of nutmeg.

3. Pour seasoned apples into the crust and top them with 4 small pats of butter

4. Put the top crust on and seal the edges well.

5. Make about 6 little cuts on the top crust with one being in the middle.

6. Place pie on a cookie sheet and bake for 20 minutes at 375 degrees. If edges are getting too brown, cover them with a ring of foil or a pie shield.

7. Bake another 20–30 minutes

8. You can also use this recipe for peaches.

9. Serve with your favorite ice cream like Caramel Swirl or Old–fashioned Vanilla.

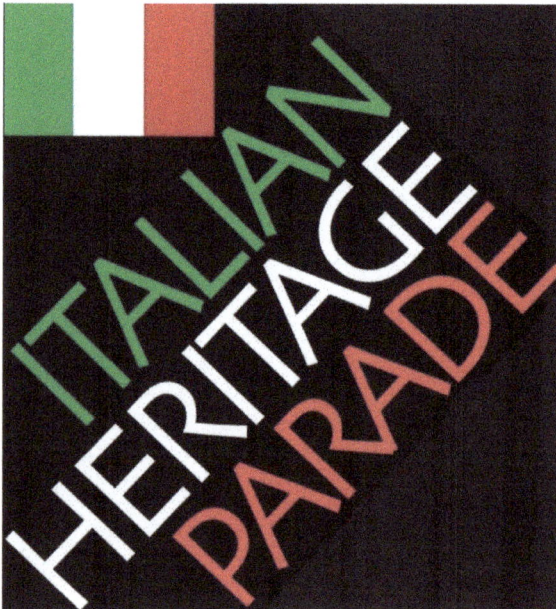

❧

COLUMBUS DAY

Christopher Columbus, at the age of 41, wrote to the King and Queen of Spain in 1492:

"Concerning the lands of India, and a Prince called Gran Khan ... How many times he sent to Rome to seek doctors in our Holy Faith to instruct him and that never had the Holy Father provided them, and thus so many people were lost through lapsing into idolatries ...

And Your Highnesses, as Catholic Christians and Princes devoted to the Holy Christian Faith ... and enemies of the sect of Mahomet and of all idolatries ... resolved to send me, Christopher Columbus, to the said regions of India, to see the said princes and peoples and lands and the dispositions of them and of all, and the manner in which may be undertaken their conversion to our Holy Faith ...

And ordained that I should not go by land (the usual way) to the Orient, but by the route of the Occident, by which no one to this day knows for sure that anyone has gone."

Columbus was looking for a sea route to India and China because 40 years earlier in 1453, the Turkish Ottoman Sultan Mehmet II conquered Constantinople, cutting off the land routes.

A biography of Columbus was written by Washington Irving in 1828, titled *A History of the Life and Voyages of Christopher Columbus.*

In it, Irving created an imaginative dialogue of Europeans arguing over whether the Earth was round or flat. His book was so popular, that people actually thought such a debate took place when it had not.

Since no ship at that time could carry enough food and water for such a long voyage, Columbus would have never set sail if he had known the actual distance.

Though Columbus was wrong about the miles and degrees of longitude, he did understand trade winds across the Atlantic.

On August 3, 1492, Columbus set sail on the longest voyage to that date out of the sight of land. Trade winds called "easterlies" pushed Columbus' ships for five weeks to the Bahamas. On October 12, 1492, Columbus sighted what he thought was India. He imagined Haiti was Japan and Cuba was the tip of China. He called the first island he saw "San Salvador" for the Holy Savior

W.L. Grant wrote in the introduction of *The Voyages and Explorations of Samuel de Champlain* (1911, Courier Press, A.S. Barnes Co):

> In the search for these were made the three greatest voyages in history, those of Columbus, of Vasco da Gama, and greatest of all of Magellan.

> In his search for the riches of Cipangu, Columbus stumbled upon America.

> The great Genoese lived and died under the illusion that he had reached the outmost verge of Asia; and though even in his lifetime men realized that what he had found was no less than a new world.

In his journal, Columbus referred to the native inhabitants as "indians" as he was convinced he had successfully arrived in India:

> So that they might be well–disposed towards us, for I knew that they were a people to be ... converted to our Holy Faith rather by love than by force, I gave to some red caps and to others glass beads ...

They became so entirely our friends that ... I believe that they would easily be made Christians.

FLOUNDER FLORENTINE

1. Sauté 1/3 of an onion finely chopped with 2 cloves of garlic in 1 teaspoon of olive oil until tender.

2. Then pour in one bag of baby spinach leaves and wilt them. Add 1/3 cup of feta or Parmesan cheese and 1 tablespoon of fresh chopped Basil and 1 tablespoon of fresh oregano leaves. Add 1/4 cup of finely diced sundried tomatoes and stir them in. Salt and pepper to taste.

3. Oil the bottom of a 13x9 inch baking dish and place one of 8 flounder filets on one side.

4. Top the filet with the spinach mixture and fold over, Flounder usually folds easily. Do this with all 8 filets lining them up next

to each other.

5. Brush the top of each filet with melted butter or olive oil and sprinkle Italian breadcrumbs over that.

6. Bake at 400 degrees for 30 minutes and check for doneness.

7. Serve over your favorite pasta, with or without sauce.

∽

MINESTRONE SOUP

1. In a large nonstick soup pot heat 1 tablespoon of olive oil over moderately high heat and add yellow onion chopped fine and 2 cloves of minced garlic and cook for 5 minutes or until onion is tender.

2. Stir in 3 ½ cups of low sodium beef broth, one 15 ounce can Great Northern beans that have been drained.

3. Add 1 ¾ cup chopped tomatoes or 1 14 ounce can of chopped Italian–style tomatoes

4. Add 2 large carrots thinly sliced and one small zucchini halved lengthwise and sliced.

5. Season with 1 teaspoon of oregano, dried or fresh and 1 teaspoon of basil dried of fresh and chopped.

6. Salt and pepper to taste.

7. Boil 10 minutes and add 2 ounce vermicelli or thin spaghetti broken.

8. Lower the heat and simmer for about 10 more minutes or until pasta is tender.

9. Serve topped with grated Parmesan cheese. Makes 8 side dish servings.

IRRESISTIBLE ITALIAN SALAD
1. Chop 1 head of Romaine lettuce and 1 head of iceberg lettuce.

2. Drain 1 can of artichoke hearts and chop small.

3. You can add one 4 ounce jar of diced pimentos or just chop cherry tomatoes.

4. Add 1/2 sliced fine red onion.

5. Top with 1/2 cup of grated Parmesan cheese, 1/2 cup of olive oil and 1/2 cup of vinegar. You can add pine nuts.

6. Salt and pepper to taste and toss all ingredients well. Serves 8.

❧

BERRY CHEESECAKE PIE

This recipe from the sisters who taught at my high school Cor Jesu Academy.

1. Make a graham cracker crust in a

glass pie dish from 2 cups of graham cracker crumbs, mixed with 1/2 cup of melted butter and 2 tablespoons of sugar.

2. Beat 2 room temperature packages of cream cheese with 2 eggs, 1/2 cup of sugar and 1 teaspoon of vanilla.

3. Bake at 375 degrees for 20 minutes.

4. Mix 1–pint sour cream with 1/2 cup of sugar and 1 teaspoon of vanilla and spread on top. Sprinkle with cinnamon.

5. Bake at 475 degrees for 5 more minutes.

6. Chill and top with your choice of fresh berries, peaches or even canned cherry pie filling.

✑
FALL FESTIVAL

" **S** ince we are surrounded by so great a cloud of witnesses, let us also lay aside every weight, and sin which clings so closely, and let us run with endurance the race that is set before us."

– Hebrews 12:1

Some prefer not to celebrate Halloween due to its pagan origins.

Catholics celebrate November 1st as All Saints Day. It began as a day to honor the martyrs of the Christian faith, designated in the 8th century by Pope Gregory III.

Protestants recognize Reformation Day, as it was on October 31, in the year 1517, that Martin Luther nailed his 95 theses, or debate questions to the door of the Wittenberg church.

The church we went to in Texas had an indoor, harvest-themed party for the children. It was fun. They played games and got prizes!

Since they did not want kids wearing scary Halloween costumes, they dressed up as Bible characters and recited Scriptures for treats. Some church members gave out cartoon Gospel tracts along with the candy.

One year, our son dressed as Moses and we made him a replica of the Ten Commandments on two wooden tablets spray painted gray. After the church party, he went around the neighborhood going to people's doors with other children. When the people inside expected a joke, our son recited all Ten Commandments in order. That was a real scare to our non-church going neighbors. They gave him as much candy as he wanted!

Let's remember the great Christians past and present who gave their lives to spread the Gospel and lead others to eternal life in Heaven. So try dressing as a Bible character and enjoy the chance to lead your neighbors to know Jesus our Savior!

❧

FUN LITTLE VEGGIE & DIP TRAY

❧

CROCK-POT PIZZA OR SPAGHETTI SAUCE

Crock-Pot Pizza or Spaghetti Sauce (My kids would want to just eat this with a spoon) It could sit on the stove to be enjoyed before and after celebrating the saints!

1. Rub olive oil around inside of Crock-Pot.

2. In a large saucepan lightly brown 1 pound ground Italian sausage and add one pound lean ground beef with 1/2 finely chopped onion and 2 cloves of garlic. Sauté until almost done. You can also add chopped green or sweet peppers.

3. Drain the grease from the meat and put the meat in the bottom of a Crock-Pot.

4. Add one large can tomato puree and on small can tomato paste. Add one can of water from the tomato paste. You can also use

Classico Tomato Basil Sauce in a jar.

5. I add 2 tablespoons of red wine, 1 teaspoon of honey, 2 tablespoons of Parmesan cheese, 1 tablespoon of sweet basil and 1 teaspoon of oregano. Salt and pepper to taste.

6. Cook on low for 4–5 hours and serve over your favorite pasta or pizza dough.

© Elizabeth LaBau

❧

AUNT LISA'S SWEET & SALTY CANDIES

A Federer Family Special Treat!

1. Line a cookie sheet with heavy duty foil. Be careful to wrap it around the sides so caramel does not stick to pan. Line the pan with saltine crackers side to side.

2. Melt 1 and 1/2 sticks of butter in a medium saucepan and add 1 +1/2 cups brown sugar and keep stirring to avoid burning. Boil hard for 3 minutes to make a caramel.

3. Pour the caramel over the crackers and bake 8 minutes at 350 degrees.

4. Remove from the oven and turn oven off

5. Sprinkle a 12 ounce package of semisweet chocolate chips evenly over all and place int the warm oven 2–3 minutes.

6. Remove pan from the oven and spread the chocolate like frosting over all the crackers and caramel.

7. I top with slivered almonds or pecans.

8. Cool in refrigerator and break into pieces.

✧

AUNT JAN'S PEANUT BUTTER BALLS
Another Federer Family Holiday Treat

1. In a soup pot melt 1 ½ stick butter. Take off heat and stir in 32 ounce peanut butter.

2. Add 1 teaspoon vanilla, 1 pound of powdered sugar (I use 1/2 powdered milk and 1/2 powdered sugar.)

3. Stir in 5 cups of Rice Krispies.

4. Shape into truffle size balls and refrigerate until set.

5. Melt 1 bag of chocolate chips and 1/2 bar paraffin wax in the microwave 1 minute

at a time and stirring in between minutes.

    6. Dip each peanut butter ball in melted chocolate with a fork.

    7. Place on wax paper and refrigerate 1 hour.

Great American Holiday Cookbook – Susie Federer

✦

VETERANS DAY–NOVEMBER 11

"As a former soldier, I am delighted that our VETERANS are sponsoring a movement to increase our awareness of God in our daily lives. In battle, they learned a great truth-that there are no atheists in the foxholes. They know that in time of test and trial, we instinctively turn to God for new courage and peace of mind. All the history of America bears witness to this truth."

–President Dwight Eisenhower, broadcast from White House for American Legion Back-to-God Program, February 7, 1954

Armistice Day was changed to VETERANS DAY in 1954 to honor all who have served defending the United States.

In 1958, President Eisenhower placed soldiers in the Tomb of the Unknown Soldier from WWII and the Korean War. In 1984, President Ronald Reagan placed a soldier from the Vietnam War in the tomb.

President Warren G. Harding stated, November 11, 1921:

On the threshold of eternity, many a soldier, I can well believe, wondered how his ebbing blood would color the stream of human life, flowing on after his sacrifice ... Standing today on hallowed ground ... it is fitting to say that his sacrifice, and that of the millions dead, shall not be in vain ...

I can sense the prayers of our people, of all peoples, that this Armistice Day shall mark the beginning of a new and lasting era of peace on earth, good will among men. Let me join in that prayer.

"Our Father who art in heaven, hallowed be Thy name. Thy kingdom come, Thy will be done on earth, as it is in heaven. Give us this day our daily bread, and forgive us our trespasses as we forgive those who trespass against us. And lead us not into temptation, but deliver us from evil, for Thine is the kingdom, and the power, and the glory, forever. Amen."

Charles Michael Province, U.S. Army, wrote:

It is the Soldier, not the minister

Who has given us freedom of religion.

It is the Soldier, not the reporter

Who has given us freedom of the press.

It is the Soldier, not the poet

Who has given us freedom of speech.

It is the Soldier, not the campus organizer

Who has given us freedom to protest.

It is the Soldier, not the lawyer

Who has given us the right to a fair trial.

It is the Soldier, not the politician

Who has given us the right to vote.

Today thank a Veteran for risking his very life to preserve our freedoms and attend a Veterans Day Memorial Service to honor those brave men! You can even take a special treat to someone in a Veterans' Home or Nursing Home to thank them for their service.

BEEF STROGANOFF

1. Marinate 1 pound of your favorite cut of beef cut into bite size chunks like stew meat in 1/4 cup red cooking wine or wine and 2

tablespoons of Worcestershire sauce.

Sprinkle Meat tenderizer on top with salt and pepper to taste and marinate at least 2 hours. You can marinate it overnight,

2. Heat 2 tablespoons of olive oil in skillet and brown just 1 or 2 minutes so meat stays tender.

3. Pour the marinade over the beef and bring to a simmer.

4. Turn off the heat and add about 1/2 cup sour cream to taste.

5. Top with fresh chopped chives and serve over stroganoff noodles.

∽

HAKAN'S PARMESAN BRUSSELS SPROUTS

This is the only way we will eat them!

1. Rinse & finely chop a bag of Brussels sprouts.

2. Heat 2 tablespoons of olive oil in a pan and add the chopped sprouts to the oil until crisp and a little browned.

3. Place them in a bowl and salt and pepper to taste.

4. Top with fresh grated Parmesan cheese.

࿐

BEET & SPINACH SALAD
This is beautiful served with stroganoff!
1. Arrange Baby spinach leaves on salad plates.
2. Top with thinly sliced beets.
3. Dress with Balsamic vinegar salad dressing.
4. Top with crumbled feta & chopped pecans.

࿐

BEST OATMEAL COOKIES
Another of Bill's favorites!
1. Preheat oven to 350 degrees.

2. Mix 1 cup of softened butter with 1 cup of brown sugar. (You can also substitute the butter with peanut butter and it turns out great).

3. Add 2 teaspoons of vanilla and 2 eggs.

4. In separate bowl combine 1 ½ cups flour with 1 teaspoon salt, 1/4 teaspoon baking soda, 1 teaspoon baking powder, and 1–2 teaspoons of ground cinnamon

5. Blend together with butter mixture and stir in 2 cups of oats, 1 cup of chocolate chips and 1 cup of raisins.

6. Use cookie scoop to place them on cookie sheet sprayed with just a little coconut oil.

7. Bake 10–12 minutes until lightly browned.

❧
THANKSGIVING DAY

"Congress ... hath thought proper ... to recommend to the several States ... a day of public and solemn Thanksgiving to Almighty God ...

That He would go forth with our hosts and crown our arms with victory ... That He would grant to His church, the plentiful effusions of Divine Grace, and pour out His Holy Spirit on all Ministers of the Gospel;

That He would bless and prosper the means of education, and spread the light of Christian knowledge through the remotest corners of the earth ...

I do therefore ... issue this proclamation ... appointing ... a day of public and solemn Thanksgiving and Prayer to Almighty God"

–Virginia Governor Thomas Jefferson, November 11, 1779

On November 11, 1620, the Pilgrims

signed the Mayflower Compact and began their Plymouth Colony.

Of the 102 Pilgrims, only 47 survived till Spring. At one point, only a half dozen were healthy enough to care for the rest.

In the Spring of 1621, the Indian Squanto came among them, and showed them how to catch fish, plant corn, trap beaver, and was their interpreter with the other Indian tribes.

Governor William Bradford described Squanto as "a special instrument sent of God for their good beyond their expectation."

Bradford added:

> The settlers ... began to plant their corn, in which service Squanto stood them in good stead, showing them how to plant it and cultivate it. He also told them that unless they got fish to manure this exhausted old soil, it would come to nothing ... In the middle of April plenty of fish would come up the brook ... and he taught them how to catch it.

Pilgrim Edward Winslow recorded in *Mourt's Relation* that in the Fall of 1621:

> God be praised we had a good increase ... Our harvest being gotten in, our governor sent four men on fowling, that so we might after a special manner

rejoice together after we had gathered the fruit of our labors.

After the Pilgrims prayed and fasted, Governor Bradford wrote:

> Afterwards the Lord sent them such seasonable showers, with interchange of fair warm weather as, through His blessing, caused a fruitful and liberal harvest, to their no small comfort and rejoicing.

> For which mercy, in time convenient, they also set apart a day of thanksgiving. By this time harvest was come, and instead of famine now God gave them plenty – for which they blessed God.

> And the effect of their particular planting was well seen, for all had – pretty well – so as any general want or famine had not been amongst them since to this day.

Decades later, a thanksgiving proclamation was issued by the Governing Council of Charlestown, Massachusetts, June 20, 1676:

> The Council has thought meet to appoint ... day of solemn Thanksgiving and praise to God ... that the Lord may behold us

as a people offering praise and
thereby glorifying Him.

A nice Thanksgiving tradition we enjoy
while sharing the big meal is to go around
the table and have everyone say what he is
thanking God for this year!

Let us all give thanks to the Lord for His
Blessings in our life today and everyday.

(Get the book, *The Treacherous World of the
16th Century & How the Pilgrims Escaped It*)

&

ROAST TURKEY WITH OLD
FASHIONED CORNBREAD STUFFING

1. In a medium saucepan, melt 3
tablespoons of butter over moderate heat.

Add 1 large yellow onion, 3–4 stalks of
celery, and 1–2 large apples chopped fine and
cook in butter for about 3–5 minutes or until
tender. Remove from heat.

2. In a very large bowl, combine 4 cups
of crumbled cornbread or 1 bag of cornbread

stuffing mix with the sautéed vegetables and apple and season with pepper to taste.

3. Add some fresh chopped parsley and chives – about 2–3 tablespoons of each to make it look festive.

4. Preheat oven to 325 degrees. Rinse a 12 pound turkey, fresh or defrosted and remove neck and giblets. Stuff and truss turkey. Place in large roasting pan brushed with oil, breast side up and brush to top of the turkey with oil. I also squeeze a little fresh lemon over turkey before oiling it.

5. Pour about 1/4 cup white wine around the turkey to steam it tenderly.

6. Make a heavy duty foil tent over the top of the turkey.

7. Roast turkey for 3 ½ hours or until thermometer registers 180 degrees Fahrenheit, basting often and recovering with foil to prevent over-browning. If necessary, uncover the last 30 minutes to get the skin crispy.

8. Bake any remaining stuffing in an oiled casserole dish next to the turkey after blending an egg into it and a little turkey broth to keep it moist. Bake the last 30 minutes with the turkey.

9. Let turkey stand 15 minutes before carving. Makes 12 servings.

❧

FEDERER'S SWEET POTATO SOUFFLE

1. Peel and cut into chunks, 5–6 medium sweet potatoes. Boil until done about 15–20 minutes and drain. Whip with mixer.

2. Add 1/3 stick butter, 2 large eggs, a pinch of brown sugar, 1 teaspoon of cinnamon, and one of cup coconut, and a squeeze of orange. Mix with mixer. Spread into a pretty casserole dish.

3. Melt another 1/3 stick of butter and stir in 1/3 cup of brown sugar and 1 cup of chopped pecans. Spread over potatoes.

4. Or just top with whole beautiful pecans and marshmallows. Bake at 350 degrees about 30 minutes until top bubbles. This tastes like dessert!

MIKE'S FAV GREEN BEAN CASSEROLE

1. Mix one 10 ounce can Cream of Mushroom soup (You can use Healthy Choice or 98 percent fat free) with 1 teaspoon of Worcestershire sauce and a dash of black pepper.

2. Add 2-3 cups of cut cooked green beans or 2 cans of Green Giant Kitchen Sliced Green Beans, drained.

3. Mix in 2/3 cup of French's French Fried Onion Rings.

4. Put in oiled casserole and bake at 350 degrees for 20 minutes.

5. Top with 2/3 cup more onion rings and bake 5–10 minutes more until crispy on top. Serves 6.

WILL'S FAVORITE PUMPKIN PIE

1. Place one 9 inch pie crust in glass pie pan and crimp edges.

2. Preheat oven to 425 degrees.

3. In large mixer bowl, combine one 16 ounce can of pumpkin (2 cups) with one 14 ounce can eagle Brand sweetened condensed milk (not evaporated milk), 2 eggs, 1 teaspoon of ground cinnamon, 1/2 teaspoon of nutmeg, 1/2 teaspoon of ground ginger and 1/2 teaspoon of salt. You can add 1/4 teaspoon of ground clove but my family prefers it without cloves.

4. Pour mixture into pie shell and bake for 15 minutes at 425 degrees.

5. Turn the oven temperature down to 350 degrees and bake about 30–35 minutes more. Cool and garnish as desired. Refrigerate leftovers.

PILGRIM PUMPKIN CAKE

Our children like this better than pie.

1. Preheat oven to 350 degrees.

2. In large mixing bowl, combine 1 box of Spice Cake Mix, one 1 pound of can of pumpkin, 2 teaspoons of baking soda, 2 eggs, and 1 cup of water. Beat 3 minutes on medium speed with a mixer.

3. Pour batter into greased and floured 13x9 inch baking dish and bake for 45 minutes.

4. Cool and frost with Cream Cheese Frosting or Pudding frosting below

5. For Cream Cheese Frosting, blend with mixer, 8 ounce cream cheese (can use light or free) 2 teaspoons of vanilla, 1/2 stick of softened butter, 1/8 cup of milk and 1 pound of powdered sugar.

6. For less sugar, blend 1 tub of whipped cream cheese with one package of vanilla or

cheesecake flavored instant pudding and 1/2 cup of milk until thick and frost over cake. This must be refrigerated.

*For chocolate cakes, you can also make a frosting of instant chocolate pudding mixed with cool whip or whipped cream cheese. Just remember to refrigerate it.

❧

EASY PUMPKIN BREAD

1. Preheat oven to 350 degrees.

2. Grease and flour 4 small bread pans or 2 large.

3. Mix 2 ¾ cup all–purpose flour with 1 ½ cups of brown sugar, 5 teaspoons of pumpkin pie spice, 1/4 teaspoon of baking soda, 1 teaspoon of salt, and 1/2 teaspoon of baking powder.

4. Add one 16 ounce can pumpkin, 1 cup of vegetable or coconut oil, 2 large eggs and beat with electric mixer on low until

all ingredients are moistened and mixture is smooth.

5. Spoon batter into prepared bread pans and spread evenly. I top mine with some beautiful pecans and sometimes a cinnamon streusel. You can also blend 4 ounces of cream cheese with an egg and 1 teaspoon of vanilla and swirl into the batter. I did 1/2 like that in the photo.

6. Bake at 350 degrees for 20 minutes for 4 small loaves and 35–40 minutes for 2 large loaves.

7. Cool on wire racks for 10 minutes and remove from pans if desired.

CASSIE'S FAVORITE SNICKERDOODLES

After Thanksgiving, every week, I make a couple batches of traditional cookies to gift to family and friends for Christmas. Following are a few of our favorites! Enjoy!

1. For all Butter Snickerdoodles, soften 3/4 cup of butter to room temperature and cream together with 1 cup of sugar, and 2 eggs at room temperature. Preheat oven to 400 degrees.

2. In a large bowl, whisk the dry ingredients: 2 ¾ cup all–purpose flour, 2 teaspoons of cream of tartar, 1 teaspoon of baking soda and 1/4 teaspoon of salt.

3. Mix the butter add egg mixture with the dry ingredients in the large bowl to make the dough.

4. Mix in a third bowl for topping: 3 tablespoons of white granulated sugar and 3 teaspoons of cinnamon.

5. Shape the dough into 1–inch sized balls and roll in the cinnamon sugar.

6. Place the cookie dough balls 2 inches apart on an ungreased cookie sheet and bake for 8–10 minutes. Cool 1–2 minutes on cookie sheet and then immediately remove and place on parchment or a wire rack to cool. Makes 24 cookies.

∽

CREAM CHEESE SNICKERDOODLES
For Cream Cheese Snickerdoodles follow the previous instructions using the following ingredients. I have also made them with Pumpkin Cream Cheese around the Holidays and that is the Best!

1. Blend together 1 cup of unsalted butter

softened to room temperature with 4 ounces of cream cheese or pumpkin cream cheese at room temperature, 1 cup of sugar, 2 large eggs and 1 teaspoon of vanilla extract.

2. Stir that into the large bowl of dry ingredients: 3 ¼ cups of flour, 1 teaspoon of cornstarch, 1 ½ teaspoon of cream of tartar, 1/2 teaspoon of baking soda, 3/4 teaspoon of salt and 1/2 teaspoon of cinnamon.

3. I top each pumpkin cream cheese cookie with a beautiful pecan before baking.

4. This recipe makes 35 cookies.

❧

MELODY'S CANDY CANE COOKIES

1. Mix together 1 cup of softened butter with 1 cup of confectioners' sugar and 1 egg in a large bowl.

2. Blend in 2 ½ cups of all–purpose flour and 1 teaspoon of salt.

3. Divide the dough in half, placing half

in another mixing bowl. Blend 1/2 teaspoon of red food coloring and 1/2 teaspoon of peppermint extract into half of the dough in one of the bowls.

4. Cover both halves with plastic wrap and chill for one hour.

5. Take one teaspoon of the red dough and shape into a 4–inch–long rope.

6. Take one teaspoon of white dough and do the same. For smoother ropes, you can roll them back and forth on a lightly sugared surface.

7. Place the ropes side by side, press together and twist and curve the top down to look like a candy cane.

8. Complete the cookies one at a time and place 2 inches apart on ungreased cookie sheet.

9. Bake 9–11 minutes. Cool 1 minute, then remove to a wire rack or parchment paper.

10. I also sprinkle a little red sugar on the red side before baking.

❧

HELLO DOLLIE COOKIES

These are easy and delicious anytime of the year!

1. Preheat oven to 350 degrees.

2. In a 13x9 inch baking dish melt 1/2 cup of butter in the oven.

3. Take the dish out of the oven and spread the melted butter evenly on the bottom of the dish.

4. Sprinkle 1 ½ cups of graham cracker crumbs over the butter.

5. Pour one 14 ounce can Eagle Brand Sweetened Condensed Milk over the cracker crumbs (Not Evaporated Milk)

6. Top with one 6 ounce bag of semisweet chocolate chips, 1 1/3 cup of flaked coconut and 1 cup of chopped pecans or walnuts. Press down.

7. Bake 25–30 minutes or until lightly

browned. Cool on countertop, then chill in the frig at least 30 minutes to set. Cut into 24 bars and store loosely covered at room temperature.

∽

NOTES

NOTES

NOTES

❧
NOTES

◈

RECIPE INDEX

Salads

Soups

Vegetables